Sara,

Happy 9th Birthday!

Love,

Grandma & Pop Pop

SNOWMAN

SNOWMAN

THE TRUE STORY OF A CHAMPION

WRITTEN BY **CATHERINE HAPKA**

ADAPTED FROM THE BOOK BY
RUTHERFORD MONTGOMERY

Aladdin
New York London Toronto Sydney New Delhi

ALADDIN

An imprint of Simon & Schuster Children's Publishing Division

1230 Avenue of the Americas, New York, New York 10020

First Aladdin hardcover edition August 2016

Copyright © 1962 by Rutherford Montgomery

Copyright renewed © 1990 by Eunice O. Montgomery

Revised text copyright © 2016 by Docutainment, LLC

Jacket photograph © 2016 by H & S Productions, LLC

All rights reserved, including the right of reproduction in whole or in part in any form.

ALADDIN is a trademark of Simon & Schuster, Inc., and related logo

is a registered trademark of Simon & Schuster, Inc.

For information about special discounts for bulk purchases, please contact

Simon & Schuster Special Sales at 1-866-506-1949 or business@simonandschuster.com.

The Simon & Schuster Speakers Bureau can bring authors to your live event.

For more information or to book an event contact the Simon & Schuster Speakers Bureau

at 1-866-248-3049 or visit our website at www.simonspeakers.com.

Jacket designed by Jessica Handelman

Interior designed by Mike Rosamilia

The text of this book was set in ArrusBT Std.

Manufactured in the United States of America 0716 FFG

2 4 6 8 10 9 7 5 3 1

Library of Congress Control Number 2016944863

ISBN 978-1-4814-7812-0

ISBN 978-1-4814-7814-4 (eBook)

CHAPTER 1

February 1956
New Holland, Pennsylvania
End of the Road

"BRING THE REST IN!" A VOICE SHOUTED.

The gray horse lifted his head from the trough where he'd been searching for stray scraps of hay. A slender teenage boy dressed mostly in black was hurrying toward the horse's head.

"Come on, big fella," the youth said, giving a yank to loosen the knot in the rope tying the gelding to the rail over the trough. Then he grabbed the horse's worn halter and gave a cluck and a tug. The clip on the ratty halter dug into the horse's face, but the gray gelding gave no protest. He was used to the small aches and pains of hard work and careless handling.

The horse followed without hurrying as the youth dragged him along the aisle of the auction barn. When the gray gelding had arrived, the place had been packed with horses of all shapes and sizes, tied side by side along both walls. People had wandered along the sunken walkway in between, occasionally stepping closer to lift a horse's hoof or to flip its lip up to look for a tattoo and to check its teeth. None of the people had bothered the gray horse, however. And now, hours later, the aisle was nearly deserted.

Boy and horse turned the corner into the center part of the building, where the horse fell into step behind four others, all workhorses like him but mostly much older and stoutly built, with the thick legs and massive necks of draft animals. One of the big drafts had a badly galled shoulder, and a black gelding's back was swayed from hard work and old age. All four showed ribs through their shaggy, unkempt coats.

The gray was showing the outline of ribs as well, and clearly hadn't been groomed in a while. But unlike the others, who plodded along without raising their heads, he looked around with interest, pricking his small ears as he passed through a gate into the narrow sales ring bordered on both sides by tall wooden bleachers. Earlier, this place had been filled with people, too. Now, only a few remained. The gray gelding met the eye of one of them, a stocky man wearing a heavy mackinaw coat and a cloth cap with the earflaps pulled down against the chill of the unheated building. But the man barely seemed to see the gray before turning to look at the rest.

As the gray horse passed him, the man spat a wad of tobacco onto the ground. "Sixty a head," he called in a raspy voice.

"Sold." Another man, sitting at the wooden desk overlooking the ring, gathered the papers lying before him. "That's all, folks."

"This way." The youth at the gray's head tugged again on his halter, leading him back out of the ring with the others. "Sorry, pal, looks like it's end of the road for you."

The parking lot at New Holland Sales Stables was already clearing out when Harry deLeyer steered his station wagon past cars, horse trailers, and Amish buggies. A few people were still loading the horses they'd bought, but Harry paid little attention to them. He had been to the auction before and knew how it worked. Every Monday, all year round, people came from near and far to buy and sell horses. There, one could find anything from enormous drafts weary from pulling a plow to sleek, spirited show horses to furry ponies; from high-headed saddlebreds to Thoroughbred ex-racers to horses whose breeding was anybody's guess. The buyers varied just as much. Amish farmers looking over the plow and buggy horses with a practiced eye. Trainers looking for a lesson horse or show horse at a bargain price. Families looking for an inexpensive pony for the kids. Many of the horses went home with such buyers, while other sales led to the area in the back known as "the kill pen." That was where the meat buyers kept the horses they purchased, loading them up at the end of the day for one final trailer ride to the canning plant.

That day it was snowy and bitterly cold, and Harry saw one of the meat buyers loading his truck as he pulled to a stop. He grimaced, partly because he knew the fate of the unlucky animals being loaded. It was very different from how he remembered things from his childhood in Holland, where a horse that had served his owners faithfully earned a pleasant retirement grazing in a sunny pasture.

Harry was also disappointed to be arriving at the sale so late. He'd had a flat tire on the long drive down from Long Island, New York. In those days, changing a tire was no simple matter—Harry had had to go to a service station for a new inner tube, which had put him far behind schedule. Now, he could see that the auction was over. That was too bad, since he'd been hoping to find a lesson horse for the stable he'd managed at an exclusive private school, the Knox School for Girls, for the past couple of years.

Still, he'd made the long drive through the snow from his home farm on Long Island all the way here to Pennsylvania. He figured he might as well take a look at what was left.

Harry climbed out of his car and stretched, his blue eyes never leaving the meat buyer's trailer. When he looked inside, the horses stood empty-eyed and resigned, no longer interested in what was going on around them.

All except one. A gray gelding was looking around, ears pricked. He was just as beat-up and dirty as the others, but there was something about him that caught Harry's attention—especially when the horse turned and met his gaze. Was Harry seeing things, or had the gelding just winked one big brown eye at him?

"I'd like to look that gray horse over," he told the meat buyer in his thick Dutch accent, nodding toward the gelding.

The buyer laughed. "You crazy? He's just a used-up farm horse."

Harry merely smiled. "Mind getting him down so I can have a look?"

The buyer shrugged and then unfastened the ramp he'd just latched. He lowered it, and before he could reach for the gray, Harry was inside grabbing the horse by the mane.

The gray gelding stepped down, stumbling halfway and sliding ungracefully to the ground. Harry let go and jumped out of the way. Although the meat buyer had already removed the halters from the horses in his truck, neither he nor Harry was particularly worried that the battered horse would try to run away, and indeed, the gray stood still once he was out.

Harry looked him over carefully. The horse stood a little more than sixteen hands by his estimation, and he was perhaps eight years old or thereabouts. He was solidly built, though certainly no draft horse despite the harness marks across his chest. Harry was surprised to note the small ears—"Arabian ears," he would call them. Other than those ears, the horse's best quality seemed to be his large, kind eyes. The rest of him showed the signs of hard work and poor care. His mane and tail were unkempt, and his hooves were chipped and dull, with only one worn-out shoe still clinging on by a couple of nails.

But he wasn't as thin as some of the horses that ended up in the buyers' kill pen, and his basic conformation was adequate. Besides, there was just something Harry liked about him. He might not be anything special, but seemed easy-going and quiet, so he might do as a lesson horse for some of the bigger girls at the Knox School. . . .

"How much do you want for him?" Harry asked the meat buyer.

The man looked surprised, but was quick to nod when Harry offered eighty dollars—ten for profit and ten for delivering the horse to Harry's farm on Long Island.

"You just bought yourself a horse, mister." The meat buyer grinned, probably thinking that Harry had just paid way too much for a useless horse.

Harry was thinking much the same thing himself. Still, he couldn't help smiling at the gray gelding as he led him back up the ramp into the trailer.

CHAPTER 2

Snowman

HARRY ARRIVED AT HOME BEFORE THE GRAY GELDING was delivered. His place was small—only five and a half acres—but he had worked hard over the past few years to build up Hollandia Farm, named for his homeland. In some ways this part of Long Island reminded him of the country-side around his hometown in Holland. For one thing, there were plenty of horses around in both places.

There were differences, though. When Harry was a child, even good show horses were supposed to earn their hay and oats working on the farm as well as jumping at the shows. Harry's father had insisted that the first Thoroughbred that Harry ever owned be trained to pull a plow or wagon as well as being ridden.

At Hollandia, none of the horses had to pull a plow. But all were expected to earn their keep in one way or another. The boarders did that just by being there—their owners paid Harry to take care of them, and sometimes to ride and train them. Some of the others were show horses, which Harry would train and show and eventually sell at a profit. The horses that weren't talented enough to be stars in the show ring became either lesson horses at the Knox School or stayed at Hollandia as livery horses that Harry rented out to people who didn't have horses of their own but wished to ride around the countryside now and then.

Harry's family met him at the door when he stepped inside. "Did you buy a horse?" his wife and two older children chorused eagerly.

Harry tousled the blond hair of his six-year-old son, Joseph, nicknamed Chef. Chef and his younger sister, Harriet, already had ponies of their own, and Harry was sure that three-year-old Marty would soon follow in their bootsteps.

"I was late getting to the auction," Harry told his family as he stomped the snow off his boots and led the way into the kitchen. "But I did buy a horse."

He glanced toward the window, wondering what they would think of that horse. The gray gelding wasn't the type they would be expecting—he wasn't the type Harry had expected himself to buy, for that matter. The lesson horses at the Knox School tended to be classy animals—they had to be, to satisfy the wealthy families of the girls who rode them. Would the gray fit in there?

"When's he coming?" Chef demanded eagerly.

"I get to ride him first!" Harriet put in.

Harry cleared his throat. "He might need some training."

"What's he look like?" Chef asked.

"A bit over sixteen hands, I'd say," Harry told them. "He has a fine head, Arabian ears, lively eyes."

"What did you pay for him?" asked Harry's wife, Johanna. Whenever Harry looked at her, with her dark hair and lively hazel eyes, he was sure she'd barely aged since the days they'd danced at carnivals and sat together in the stands of local horse shows back in Holland, despite the hard work of raising three active children and helping to run the busy farm.

Harry grinned at her. "Eighty dollars."

"Eighty bucks?" Chef echoed in disbelief.

Harriet looked just as surprised. "What is he, some old farm nag?" she asked.

"It's up to you two to help train him," Harry told the older children. "We have to make a riding horse out of him, or we can't keep him."

Just then came the sound of a large truck pulling into the yard. "He's here!" Chef cried, dashing toward the kitchen door with Harriet on his heels.

Harry, Johanna, and little Marty followed them out

into the snow-dusted yard. Big, fat flakes were still floating down from the gray clouds.

"Come and get him," the truck driver called as he hopped down from the cab and hurried around to the ramp. "I need to get back on the road in case this storm gets worse."

Harry nodded and stepped forward to help, holding up a hand to keep the children out of the way. Together, he and the driver lowered the ramp and fetched Harry's horse out from among the others packed inside. The gray gelding stumbled clumsily down the ramp, just as he'd done at the sales stable. Then he stood at the bottom, small ears pricked curiously toward the family watching him.

Harry winced; the horse looked even more battered and worn-down than he'd remembered. Both front legs sported ugly sores, which Harry had seen at the auction, but there also appeared to be several fresh scrapes and cuts after the crowded trailer ride. He was glad the poor thing was quickly being coated with a blanket of falling snow.

"He looks like—" Harriet began.

"A snowman!" Chef shouted with a laugh.

Johanna smiled. "What a wonderful name for him." She glanced at her husband. "If he doesn't already have a name, that is?"

"No name," Harry replied.

"Snowman, Snowman!" Chef and Harriet chanted, with little Marty joining in.

"Run and get a halter," Harry told Chef.

As the boy dashed off toward the stable, the truck driver slapped snow from his gloves. "He's all yours, then," the man said. "I'll be on my way."

Snowman didn't flinch as the truck roared to life and pulled out of the yard. Once it was gone, the gray horse shook himself like a dog, probably trying to dislodge the snow coating his body.

"Here's a halter!" Chef cried, racing back into the yard, all out of breath. "I think this one'll fit Snowman, right, Dad?"

"Let's see." Harry took the halter and slipped it onto the gray horse's head.

Meanwhile, Chef rubbed some snow off Snowman's shoulder. His hand came away black with dirt, and he wrinkled his nose.

Then Snowman lowered his head toward Chef until the two of them were eye to eye. Chef gasped.

"He just winked at me!" he exclaimed.

Harry chuckled, remembering that he'd had that same impression at the auction. Maybe this Snowman would turn out to have some life left in him after all. At the very least, he seemed to be a character.

"Probably just a snowflake in his eye," he told Chef with a grin.

Harriet stepped forward to rub a patch of snow off

Snowman's other shoulder. "We'll make a fine horse out of you, Snowman," she told the big gray softly.

Harry was smiling at his daughter, thinking how much she reminded him of himself at her age, when a flurry of movement caught his eye. Looking down, he saw that Marty had just slipped past Chef and wrapped his small arms around one of Snowman's forelegs.

"Marty, no!" Johanna yelped, leaping forward as the toddler squealed with delight and squeezed even harder.

Many horses would have been startled at being grabbed that way. Some might have kicked out or jumped back, knocking Marty head over heels, perhaps injuring him badly—or worse.

But not Snowman. He stood solid as a rock, moving only to lower his head and nuzzle the little boy's bright blond hair.

He remained still even when Johanna yanked Marty away. "Look at you!" she scolded the little boy. "You're covered with dirt. I'll have to change your clothes."

Marty smiled at her, lifting one chubby fist to rub at a smudge of dirt on one of his cheeks. "Snowman!" he cried, and then tried to pull away from his mother.

Harry chuckled, relieved that nothing bad had happened—and impressed anew with the gray horse. "Better take the little ones inside," he told his wife. "Snow's coming down harder."

Johanna nodded, leading away a protesting Marty and an even more reluctant Harriet. But Chef trailed along behind his father as Harry led Snowman into the tidy barn.

Harry's head was full of plans for training the gray gelding. His goal was to win Snowman's trust and affection if possible, without spoiling him. Snowman would be expected to work hard in his new life as a lesson horse, and he would need to be reliable and safe for students of all levels if he was to earn his keep.

"But first things first," Harry told Chef as he led Snowman into his new stall. "We need to make poor old Snowman look like a horse again."

CHAPTER 3

The Makeover

OVER THE NEXT FEW DAYS AND WEEKS, SNOWMAN'S makeover became a family project, like most things around Hollandia Farm. Whenever they headed out to the barn, all five deLeyers slipped on wooden clogs from the mat outside the kitchen door. That was what Harry and Johanna had worn in their early years in Holland, and they'd never found anything better for working around the stables.

The deLeyers shampooed and rinsed Snowman over and over until they'd washed the last bits of grime and smell out of his coat and skin. It was wintertime, which meant heating bucket after bucket of water with a plug-in heating coil and drying every inch of the big gray horse with towels. Once the gelding was clean enough, Harry pulled out the horse clippers to trim Snowman's whiskers and fetlocks, and then Harriet and Chef helped curry and brush every inch of Snowman's body, loosening the dead hair and whisking away embedded dust until finally his pale coat began to shine. They also worked all the knots and brambles out of his mane and tail, then combed and conditioned them. The farrier came to trim the horse's neglected hooves and shoe him. And of course, Harry doctored the sores on the gelding's legs, which soon looked much better. But no amount of doctoring or grooming made much difference in the marks left by the heavy work harness he'd once worn. Harry suspected those marks might always be visible.

Slowly, day by day, Snowman became a different horse. He eagerly cleaned up the hay and grain Harry fed him, and the good food filled out his ribs and topline. He remained as calm and unruffled as ever, but he showed more signs of life and energy with each passing day.

One afternoon, Harry stood in the barn with Johanna as they watched Chef and Harriet hard at work on Snowman's daily grooming. He was pleased with what he saw. Snowman might never be mistaken for a Thoroughbred, but he no longer resembled a broken-down workhorse, either. His neck was arched, his coat gleamed from grooming and good health, and his eyes were bright and interested in life. Harry couldn't help thinking that the big horse was like a tramp who'd finally had the chance to clean up and put on decent clothes.

"He's so sensible and quiet, he should make a good

lesson horse at the school," Harry mused, thinking aloud. "He might not be fancy, but he'll be perfect for timid beginners, and he's stout enough to carry even the biggest girls."

Johanna glanced over at him. "I think Chef and Harriet have plans for keeping him here at Hollandia," she said with a smile. "They're very fond of him. Marty likes him too."

Harry chuckled. "I'm in the horse business, remember?" he said. "Here at Hollandia, nobody would be interested in renting a plow horse to ride. But at the school, they won't mind as long as he can do the job." He winked at his wife. "Remember how my father always said that every horse we owned had to earn his feed?"

Johanna smiled and nodded. Then she turned to watch the children. Harriet was working on one side with a brush, Chef on the other with a currycomb.

Harry watched the children work too. "I wish I could get them that interested in the station wagon," he joked. "It needs washing and polishing."

"I remember how you acted when you were their age," Johanna said playfully. "You were much more interested in horses than cars too. Didn't you ride a winner at the fair when you were only nine?"

"I would've washed Father's new truck if the Germans hadn't grabbed it a few weeks after he bought it. We were all very proud of that new Ford truck." Harry stepped forward. "Guess I'd better start working Snowman before the kids wear him out with their brushing and combing."

At that moment Marty came rushing out of the tack room. He had hay in his hair and was carrying a bridle, the bit clanking and the reins trailing behind and threatening to trip him as he ran toward Snowman's stall.

"Wanna ride?" he shouted.

Harry stopped him with a firm hand on the shoulder. "Put that bridle back where you found it," he told his youngest child sternly. "You'll get your chance to ride Snowman—but only after we teach him a few things."

Marty glared up at his father. None of the children disobeyed Harry when he took that tone, but sometimes they couldn't resist testing him—at least a little.

"Wanna ride," Marty muttered defiantly, swinging the bridle back and forth. Then he turned and trudged back toward the tack room.

Only then did Harry allow himself to smile. He loved seeing his children so interested in horses, just as he loved seeing a horse enjoy his job. But in both cases, it was best to remain firm and even a little tough—but always with an underlying love and affection.

He soon set that philosophy to work in Snowman's training. That first day, he asked Chef to help him lay out a course of wooden jump poles. Instead of hanging the poles between standards as usual, they instead laid them directly on the ground.

"The only thing we really know about Snowman's past is that he worked as a plow horse," Harry told his son as they dragged more poles into the riding ring. "And the first thing a plow horse has to learn, if he's to become a reliable riding horse, is sure-footedness."

"'Sure-footedness'?" Chef echoed.

Harry nodded. "There's no telling what obstacles or hazards a horse might encounter on a trail or even a riding ring," he said. "Do you remember how Snowman stumbled coming down the trailer ramp?"

Chef remembered. "Probably only because of the snow," he guessed.

"We'll see."

When their course of ground poles was ready, Harry fetched Snowman and led him over the course at a walk, with Chef and Harriet watching from nearby. "Oh no!" Harriet exclaimed the first time the gray horse stumbled over a pole.

"Careful, Snowman!" Chef added.

But Snowman continued to amble along, paying little attention to where his big feet went. Poles flipped and scattered as the horse made his clumsy way around the ring. By the end, Harriet and Chef looked worried.

"Is he okay, Daddy?" Harriet asked.

Harry didn't respond to her question. "Hold him for me, please, Harriet." He handed her the lead rope. "Come, Chef. Let's set it up again."

Moments later the course was restored. Harriet handed over Snowman's lead, and she and her brother took their places at the edge of the ring.

Harry smiled at Snowman as he gave a light tug on the lead. "Ready to try it again, Snowman?" he asked.

The second time through, Snowman did better—at least a little. He seemed to understand that a flipped pole could hurt when it rapped his legs. Still, he ended up scattering quite a few poles by the end.

As he finished, Harriet let out a wail of dismay. "He's so clumsy he'll throw off every one of those Knox girls!" she cried. Stomping closer, she shook a finger at the big gray horse. "Pick up your feet, Mr. Clumsy!"

"Just imagine what would happen if he tried to canter around the course," Chef said with a laugh.

"Straighten out the poles, son," Harry told him.

All Snowman did that first day was walk. But Harry repeated the exercise day after day, and before long, the gray horse began to lift his feet and space his steps to avoid the poles. After a while Harry taught him to trot over the poles, and eventually, Snowman was able to canter along and never touch a pole.

Meanwhile, his training continued in other ways, too. Harry found a saddle for Snowman and tacked him up, leaning over Snowman's back to teach him the feel of having a person on his back. The horse seemed confused but agreeable about the whole ordeal, so Harry soon moved on to riding, teaching Snowman basic cues to fill out what he already knew from his plow horse days. The horse had such a steady temperament that it wasn't long before Harriet was allowed to ride him, and then Chef.

When Chef could gallop the big gray safely around the ring, it was finally little Marty's turn. "Quiet now, son," Harry said as he lifted the little boy into the saddle. "Snowman is still learning, all right?"

"Go, Snowman!" Marty cried, kicking his small heels against the horse's sides and pounding on Snowman's withers with his pudgy hands. "Let's gallop!"

Harry's hand moved toward the horse's bridle, ready to grab it if Snowman took off. But he needn't have worried. The big gray flicked an ear back toward the little boy and then stepped off at a sedate walk. He plodded calmly around the ring, ignoring Marty's shouts to move faster, and Harry smiled.

Yes, Snowman would do nicely as a lesson horse.

CHAPTER 4
Harry's History

ONE MORNING, HARRY STOOD WITH JOHANNA AND watched the horses in the main pasture at Hollandia Farm. Snowman was grazing off a little by himself, ignoring the rest of the herd. He got along with other horses well enough—from the calm rental plugs to the more high-spirited show animals—but always seemed to prefer the company of people.

Suddenly, one of the Thoroughbreds let out a snort and a buck and then took off galloping around the pasture. Most of the others joined in, but Snowman merely lifted his head briefly before returning to his grazing.

"Once a plow horse, always a plow horse," Harry said with a smile.

"You know better than that," Johanna responded. "Don't you remember those two plow horses on the tobacco farm?"

Harry certainly did remember those horses. "Those days weren't easy, were they?" he murmured, thinking back.

It had all started in the days of the Second World War, when a teenaged Harry had befriended several American soldiers stationed near his hometown. The soldiers had been homesick for the United States and had been happy to tell Harry all about their beloved homeland. Many of the stories had involved happy days on lush, endless farms with acres of corn blowing in the breeze. It had sounded like paradise to Harry!

The reality had been a little different. The war had ended, and Harry and Johanna had been newly married when they'd boarded a Dutch ship called the *Westerforn*. The long sea journey had been their honeymoon, and they'd both looked forward to their new lives in their new homeland.

They'd arrived with only their life savings of one hundred and eighty dollars, which Harry used to get started in his new job as a sharecropper. That meant he would farm another man's land, and instead of paying a lease fee, the landowner would receive 50 percent's worth of each year's crop. It had seemed like a wonderful opportunity to the young Dutch couple. The tobacco farm in North Carolina was so big that it made the little farms back home in Holland look like garden plots. The soil was black and rich enough to grow anything.

That first year, Harry had worked harder than ever before, chopping weeds out of the tobacco rows and driving a cultivator pulled by two placid, old draft horses. At the same time, Johanna had turned the small sharecropper's shack into a home, sewing curtains and stuffing cushions.

Despite all the hard work, Harry hadn't been able to resist spending a little of his precious free time on his true passion: training horses. He'd taught one of the chunky old drafts to jump a little, even winning ten dollars in the local village horse show. The farm owner frowned upon such foolishness, but Harry was such a hard worker that the man didn't bother to complain.

Life had been hard but good, at least for that first summer. But when harvesttime came, the tobacco crop was a complete failure. Harry got 50 percent of nothing, and his life savings were gone too, used up in living expenses. What's more, he and Johanna were by then expecting their first child, due to arrive in about three months.

The tobacco farmer couldn't afford to advance the deLeyers enough money for another year, and so Harry had to find another way to earn a living. By that time, Johanna's sister had also immigrated to America, and they'd gone to stay with her while Harry searched for a job. He'd hoped to find work with horses, his true talent and interest. But he'd looked everywhere, knowing that babies cost money and willing to do whatever he could to support his young family.

The only job he'd been able to find right away was working in a dairy. It was far from his dream job, but it paid the bills—barely. To help make ends meet, Harry also took on any part-time jobs he could find to earn a little extra money. Eventually, he even saved up enough to buy an ancient car, which was in such a state of disrepair that Johanna had to hold a flashlight out the window when they drove at night because the headlights didn't work. Harry couldn't afford to buy parts to fix the lights—not with a baby on the way.

Soon, Chef was born, and while the birth went smoothly, the hospital bills ate up all the rest of their meager savings. They didn't even have enough money left to buy an airmail stamp to rush the news to their family back in Holland!

But the new parents were thrilled with their baby boy. And Chef wasn't the only good thing to happen that week. Just days before the birth, Harry had received a telegram offering him a job working with horses!

"The owner of the stable is a fellow named William Stirling," Harry had told Johanna eagerly at the time. "He heard about me from Mickey Walsh."

"Who's Mickey Walsh?" Johanna asked.

"A shrewd judge of men and horseflesh." Harry smiled. "He saw me ride in a show when we were still at the tobacco farm. I reckon he liked my way with a horse."

Johanna had laughed then. "Yes—especially since the horse in question was used to pulling a plow, not jumping!"

Harry grinned at her, feeling happy about this new turn of events. Mickey Walsh was a very important horseman at the time—a leading steeplechase trainer who'd won countless ribbons on the big-time jumper circuit in his younger days. Besides that, he was an immigrant like Harry, though he'd come from Ireland rather than Holland.

"In any case, Mr. Walsh advised me to stick with jumpers," Harry added. "It was only bad luck that I ended up with black-and-white cows instead!"

But now Harry's luck was changing. The whole family moved to western Pennsylvania for Harry's new job. Mickey Walsh had told Harry's new boss that Harry had quite a bit of experience with hunters and jumpers. That was true enough, even if Harry had been focusing more on tobacco and dairy cows at the time. Harry had started riding at four years old and showing at nine. He'd been a member of the junior Dutch Olympic team and had competed across Europe, and in 1949, he'd placed third in an international show in Belgium.

Even so, he knew he had a lot to learn about training horses as a business. And working with Bill Stirling at Stirrup Hill Farm gave him the chance to learn just that. So did his next job, showing and training show horses for a wealthy Virginia businessman.

He'd enjoyed working with the fine, well-bred show horses on both farms. But he'd also bought and trained his own horses on the side. He mostly sought out unmanageable horses at bargain-basement prices and then used patient handling and expert training to get them over their bad habits so he could resell them at a profit. Before long, word got around about how good Harry was, and owners came to Harry with their most challenging horses. One of those horses was Sinjon, a failed racehorse and talented jumper that'd proved himself notoriously unreliable on course. Until Harry came along, nobody was willing to take him over jumps and risking an embarrassing refusal at best, a bad fall at worst. But in Harry's hands, Sinjon became a reliable and valuable show horse that would eventually compete in the Olympics. Harry couldn't compete, however, because he was a professional trainer and rider, and the Olympics was only for amateurs. Still, he got to see a horse he'd trained take part in this and other prestigious competitions.

Finally, Harry had saved up enough to start Hollandia Farm, where he had bought, trained, and sold many horses. He had a good job at the Knox School. His latest project, a fine little mare named Wayward Wind, was showing promise as a show jumper. He had a good reputation among the horse folk in his corner of Long Island, and his family was happy.

Harry couldn't help feeling thankful for all he had as he stood beside his wife watching the horses. But his gaze kept wandering back to Snowman, still grazing quietly on his own. The big gray was like no other horse Harry had ever owned. There was nothing especially distinguished or notable about him. He was just a plow horse that had learned to carry a rider.

But even then, to Harry deLeyer, he was somehow something special.

CHAPTER 5

The Knox School and Beyond

"ARE YOU SURE HE HAS TO GO?" HARRIET ASKED plaintively as Harry led Snowman out of the barn one day.

Chef reached out to stroke the big gray's side as he walked past. "We'll miss you, Snowman."

"You won't have time to miss him," Harry told the children. "We've got plenty of other horses here to take care of."

Chef shrugged. "I'll still miss Snowman."

Harry didn't answer. In the horse business it didn't pay to get too attached to the horses. His children would learn that soon enough. For instance, it had been difficult for Harry to let Sinjon go after forging such a close relationship with him, but that had been the best thing for both of them. And it would be the best thing for Snowman too. Harry was sure that the big, calm gray would perform well in his new job as a lesson horse. With any luck one of the girls who rode him would fall in love with Snowman and decide to buy him.

He gave the horse a pat. "I'll miss you too, Snowman," he murmured when he was sure the children weren't listening.

Soon, Snowman was settled in his new stall at the Knox School for Girls. By then, the big gray was well-muscled and fit from his time at Hollandia Farm, his coat gleaming with good health. Only the faint remains of those harness marks belied his true origins, though most of the girls who rode him didn't even notice the marks.

The Knox School had been in business for fifty-two years at that point. Thousands of girls had received a good education there, including the daughters of the rich, famous, and powerful. The school stood amid rolling, wooded hills, with its own beach along with meadows and thickets that, in the spring, were aflame with dogwood blossoms.

Harry was in charge of the school's well-appointed stables, where he taught many girls to ride. Some of the girls taught him a few things in return. They loved to tease him about his Dutch accent, and a few girls even offered to help him improve his English. Harry enjoyed their lessons—even when he discovered that they'd taught him a few four-letter words that definitely weren't suitable for the genteel atmosphere of the Knox School!

Riding was one of the many skills the Knox girls were expected to learn as part of the proper education of wealthy young ladies. However, only a few of them had a real interest in horses, and many of those already had well-bred horses of their own that they boarded at the school.

Many girls rode Snowman during his first year at the Knox School. He became quite popular, especially with the larger or more timid riders. He performed his job expertly and calmly, whether his rider wanted to hack out on the miles of wooded trails surrounding the school or just walk and trot around in the ring. Harry watched all the girls with Snowman, wondering who might be the first to fall in love with, and insist on buying, the big, steady gray.

But it never happened. All the riders liked Snowman, but none ever mentioned wanting to make him her own. Harry suspected most of the riders at the school would never be interested in developing a personal attachment to any horse. Their minds were occupied by other things.

Finally, he gave up, accepting that Snowman would be coming back to Hollandia Farms at the end of the school year. When the big gray gelding arrived home in the spring of 1957, he pricked his ears at the familiar surroundings, seeming happy to be back. Chef and Harriet were happy too, leading Snowman out to the pasture and staying there to watch him settle in.

Harry smiled as he and Johanna watched from the gate, but he felt worried as he tried to figure out what to do next. Johanna saw his expression.

"What is it?" she asked. "Aren't you glad to have him home?"

Harry met her eye. "You know I'm attached to Snowman," he said. "Sort of the way a man might get attached to a fine collie. But the moment he sets foot on the place, he becomes a loss in the farm's account book."

Johanna leaned on the fence, watching as the children frolicked with the big horse. "I'm sure you can find a job for him."

"No, what I need to find is a buyer." Harry sighed. "But who is going to want a plow horse that is now a safe but hardly exciting riding horse?"

He did his best to find such a buyer, and eventually, one came along. Dr. Rugen was a neighbor who lived six miles from Hollandia. His son, Richard, occasionally came by to take a riding lesson from Harry or help around the farm, and the doctor had recently decided it was time for the boy to have a horse of his own. Harry had originally promised to sell him a particular horse, but had forgotten and sold that horse to someone else. But now he had the perfect substitute in mind: Snowman.

The doctor climbed out of his car and looked over the paddocks and stable. His expression was interested but cautious. When Harry came out of the tack room, the doctor smiled uncertainly.

"Hello, Mr. deLeyer," he said. "I hope this new horse is

as nice as the other one. And I hope he's safe. I don't want to worry when my boy goes riding." He watched one of the show horses trot across the paddock, tossing his head. "I don't want an animal that prances around. From what I've observed, most riding horses prance and are flighty."

"Hmm," Harry said.

"Yes, and I might want to take a ride at times myself," the doctor added. "So it must be a well-behaved creature." He looked at Harry questioningly. "So where is this Snowman you mentioned? Will you guarantee that he's gentle?"

"I'll guarantee him." Harry knew there were few true guarantees when it came to horses, but this was a promise he felt confident in making. "Come with me."

He told the doctor to wait and then went to fetch Snowman from his stall. If this sale worked out, it could be the ideal solution for his problem. The doctor was a pleasant man—one who was likely to treat a horse in his care very well. If he liked Snowman, it meant the big gray would have a useful life at the Rugens' farm. Besides that, it meant he would be remaining in the area, and Harry and his family might even get to see him once in a while.

"Here he is," he announced as he led Snowman toward the nearest empty paddock. "I'll let him loose so you can get a look at him."

Snowman turned and eyed the doctor as he passed. When Harry turned him out into the paddock, Snowman ambled off a few steps from the gate and then broke into an easy trot.

Dr. Rugen watched him with interest. After a few moments Harry whistled, and Snowman turned and trotted over to him, thrusting his big gray head over the fence for a scratch.

"He's a fine family horse," Harry said, giving Snowman a pat instead of a scratch for once. That was because Snowman enjoyed head scratches so much that he almost always rolled his upper lip in pleasure, baring his teeth in a grimace that the doctor might have misunderstood.

"Pretty large animal," the doctor said, peering up at the horse. "But he looks safe enough. How much do you want for him?"

Harry swallowed hard. On the one hand, he was relieved that the doctor seemed to care only about Snowman's amiable temperament and not his pedigree or accomplishments. He was also relieved that Dr. Rugen didn't seem to hold a grudge about losing the other horse Harry had promised to sell him.

On the other hand, Harry realized he would miss the big gray gelding. Somehow, Snowman had wormed his way into Harry's heart in a way that few other horses ever had.

Still, he knew he had to think like a businessman, or he'd soon have a farm full of useless horses. How often did a buyer come along looking for a horse like Snowman?

"One hundred and sixty dollars," he told the man. That was less than the other horse had sold for, but twice what Harry had paid for Snowman at the auction—a good profit for a former plow horse in Harry's estimation. "But," he couldn't help adding, "if you ever sell him, it must be back to me. I'll pay you what you pay me for him."

The doctor smiled eagerly, clearly comforted by the money-back guarantee. "It's a deal!" he said, sticking out his hand for Harry to shake.

And just like that, Snowman had a new home.

CHAPTER 6

The Doctor's Farm

SOON, DR. RUGEN LEFT IN HIS CAR TO LET HIS SON know about their new horse. Harry had promised to haul Snowman over to the man's house in a little while. First, he knew his family would want to say good-bye.

As soon as the doctor's car had disappeared, they came pouring out of the house. When Harriet heard the news, she looked stricken, and Chef kicked at a stone on the ground. But neither uttered a word of complaint. After growing up in the horse business, they knew better.

Instead, they set about making a fuss over Snowman. The gelding perked up at the attention, stamping his foot and jerking on the lead rope Harry was holding, as if demanding to be turned loose so he could run around and show off.

Harry tugged firmly on the rope. "No run today," he told Snowman gruffly. "You're going for a ride in a little while."

"Is that doctor a nice man?" Harriet asked anxiously.

"Very nice," Harry assured her. "His son will be good to Snowman, don't worry."

"He knows how to take care of a horse, then?" Johanna asked with a small frown.

Harry hesitated. He'd been so eager to make what had seemed like the perfect sale that he realized he hadn't really questioned the man much. Still, he was sure it would work out. And at least Snowman was near enough that Harry could keep an eye on him and offer advice if the doctor seemed to be in over his head. Everyone had to learn about horses somehow, and Snowman would be a good teacher—of that Harry felt certain.

"He has enough pasture and a barn for winter shelter," he told his wife. "I'll explain to his boy about grain and grooming and such."

Just then he spotted a flurry of movement out of the corner of his eye. Looking that way, he saw that little Marty had slipped around behind Snowman while they were talking. He was jumping up and down, grabbing at Snowman's flowing white tail—and laughing with delight when he caught hold and hung on.

Harry's heart skipped a beat, but Snowman didn't budge except to look around curiously at the little boy. In two quick steps Harry reached Marty and pulled him away.

"Never do that again," he scolded the boy sharply as he set him beside Johanna. "Other horses will kick."

"Not our Snowman," Harriet said, her lip quivering slightly.

Chef cleared his throat. "At least we'll still be able to see him some," he told his sister bravely. "We can ride over to the doctor's place once in a while."

"A good idea," Harry agreed. "Now, say your good-byes, and Snowman and I will be on our way."

Johanna and Harriet took turns hugging the big gray. Chef didn't want to seem sentimental, so he merely gave Snowman a pat and a gruff good-bye. Meanwhile, Marty was clamoring to ride, so Harry swung him onto Snowman and let him sit there bareback while he led Snowman across the yard to the trailer, which was already hitched to his pickup.

Then Harry lifted Marty down, and the family stood watching while he loaded Snowman. The big gray stepped into the trailer almost eagerly, as if he was looking forward to the ride. Harry cleared his throat again, which suddenly seemed to have a lump in it. He'd said good-bye to many a nice horse over the years, but he'd never felt this sentimental about the partings before, not even with Sinjon and the other fancy show jumpers. How could he feel this way about a plain, easygoing gray gelding that'd never really done much of anything? Well, except make his personality felt, that is.

"It won't be the same around here," Chef said sadly as he watched. "That Snowman was sure a real clown."

Harry had never thought about it that way before, but he realized his son had put his finger on it exactly. Snowman was a horse with a sense of humor.

Snowman was also an intelligent horse, and it didn't take him long to figure out that life at the doctor's place was different from what it had been at Hollandia Farm and the Knox School's stables. It wasn't bad, exactly, but he missed his daily grooming and the frequent attention of Harry and his family. Being at the doctor's was like being back on the farm where he'd lived before the auction, except that he didn't have a lot of hard work to do.

In fact, he had little work to do at all. The doctor's son rode him occasionally, but the placid gray wasn't exciting enough for the boy, especially compared to the fiery beasts he'd seen others riding around the neighborhood.

The doctor rode a time or two himself, but quickly decided he had little interest in horseback riding. Soon, Snowman was left to exercise himself in the pasture, with only birds and other local wildlife for company most of the time. The doctor or his son would feed the gray horse, but neither lingered long in the barn to pay attention to him. That was difficult for a horse that liked human companionship, and Snowman spent the winter feeling bored, lonely, and restless.

One spring morning the doctor was driving out of his yard when his next-door neighbor hurried out to flag him down. The man's face was red, and he was scowling.

The doctor stopped, wondering if his neighbor was feeling ill and in need of his professional services. But when the neighbor approached the car, he gave the doctor a cold stare.

"I have something to show you," he said grimly.

"Where?" the doctor asked, perplexed by his neighbor's belligerent tone.

"At my place."

The doctor reached across to open the passenger-side door. "Get in," he said. "I'll drive you over there."

The neighbor's home was set among spacious, impeccably landscaped grounds surrounded by a high stone wall with a wrought-iron gate. He directed the doctor to stop in front of the gate, which was closed.

"Come with me," he said tersely, jumping out of the car.

Dr. Rugen was more puzzled than ever as he followed his neighbor toward the gate. As the man opened it and led the way through, the doctor looked around. The first thing he noticed was the deep imprints of a horse's hooves crisscrossing the otherwise flawless lawn. Nearby, a bed of asters and tulips had been trampled, and the top of a budding spirea bush appeared to have been nibbled half away.

Now that he had a horse, the doctor guessed that the

neighbor must consider him some kind of equine expert. "It would appear you have been visited by a stray horse," he said. Glancing toward the stone wall, he added, "I take it that your gate was left open?"

This seemed a reasonable deduction to him, since the stone wall was more than four feet high and a least two feet wide at the top.

"The gate was closed and latched," the neighbor replied firmly. "It always is because it works by a spring that closes it."

"Impossible," the doctor declared. "There's no other way a horse could get into this place."

"My dog awakened me this morning," his neighbor said grimly. "When I went to the window, I saw him chasing a gray horse. That horse jumped out of the yard—right over the stone wall." Perhaps noting the doctor's raised eyebrows, he added, "My wife saw it too."

"A gray horse?" the doctor echoed, still wondering why the neighbor had accosted him to tell him this wild tale.

"Your horse!" the neighbor almost shouted. "It was *your* horse, Rugen! We watched him run across the road and down to your pasture. He jumped back in over your fence."

"What? Impossible!" the doctor exclaimed, completely bewildered now. "That horse couldn't jump over a log in the road. I know— I've ridden him on several occasions myself and could barely get him to move!"

"If it happens again, I'll call the sheriff's office," the neighbor said, glaring at the doctor.

"I'm sorry" was all the doctor could think to reply. "DeLeyer never told me that horse was a jumper. He actually guaranteed that he wouldn't jump around or act silly."

"No matter; he jumps." The neighbor turned and stomped off toward his house.

"I'll pay for the damages," the doctor called after him.

The neighbor paused and looked back, his expression softening slightly. "That's not necessary," he said gruffly. "Just raise that fence of yours a foot or two."

He hurried the rest of the way to the house, slamming the door after him. The doctor stood in the yard for another moment or two, staring at the big hoofprints in the lawn. Then, shaking his head, he opened the gate—the spring had shut it firmly behind them—and headed back to his car.

CHAPTER 7

Good Fences Make
Good Neighbors

HARRY WAS SURPRISED WHEN DR. RUGEN CALLED him one day out of the blue. He was even more surprised by the man's question: "Is that Snowman horse you sold me a jumper?"

"No," Harry said immediately. "When I got him he had trouble stepping over a few poles scattered on the ground."

The doctor let out a loud sigh. "Thanks," he said, sounding relieved. "That's what I thought."

He hung up, and Harry spent a moment thinking fondly about Snowman and his days at Hollandia. Then he went about his business, forgetting about the odd call completely.

Several mornings later he got up early as he always did. He slipped into his wooden shoes and headed across the yard toward the stable to take care of the morning feeding and chores. Birds were singing in the trees bordering the paddocks, and a fresh breeze was blowing in from the nearby fields.

The breeze carried the horsey scent of the stable and paddocks to Harry, and he smiled and breathed in deeply. This was a time of day he thoroughly enjoyed. It was just him and the horses and—

His mind stalled in midthought as he got his first good look into the nearest paddock. He stared, hardly believing his eyes.

A gray horse was frolicking around the enclosure, kicking up his heels and shaking his head playfully. Harry blinked. It was Snowman!

"How did you get in there?" he murmured. His eyes darted from the gate, which was closed and latched, to the perimeter of the fence, which was solid—with no missing rails or other breaks.

Stepping closer, Harry let out a whistle. Snowman whirled around and spotted him. With a happy nicker, he loped over to meet him at the gate.

Harry rubbed the big gray head, mystified. Finally, he laughed.

"Well," he said, and shook his head.

Snowman nickered again. Harry scratched his neck, sinking his fingers deep. Snowman curled his upper lip in a happy grimace, baring his teeth. It was obvious that he was happy to be home.

Then Harry stepped back and studied the situation. How

had Snowman arrived here? If the doctor had brought him, Harry was sure the man would have knocked on the door.

No, it was obvious that the horse had brought himself home. Harry turned his gaze to the gray's powerful hindquarters as he recalled the doctor's strange phone call from the other day. Was it possible? Could Snowman have jumped out of the doctor's pasture and then into this paddock here in Hollandia?

"No," he whispered. "Maybe . . ."

He shook his head again, hardly daring to imagine it. Horses rarely jumped unless they'd been taught. Especially over an obstacle as high as his paddock fence!

But one thing was indisputable: Snowman had returned. Harry had to figure out how it had happened.

He patted the big gray's neck. "I'd better look into this," he said, and then turned toward the house.

At the kitchen door he kicked off his wooden shoes and then went through the kitchen into the living room. He sat beside the phone table and looked up the Rugens' number. Moments later, the doctor answered.

"This is deLeyer calling," Harry said. "I have your horse here in my paddock."

"Yes, my horse is gone!" The doctor sounded furious. "And after I paid handsomely to have my pasture fence raised an entire foot, too!"

"Oh." Harry thought back again to that first phone call.

"I've already had three calls from angry potato farmers in my neighborhood," the doctor continued, his voice crackling with anger. "That horse damaged a lot of potato plants! He charged around in at least three fields. The state police are on their way to investigate."

Harry hesitated. "I think it must have been an accident," he said without much conviction. "I never taught that horse to jump. I've never even seen him step over anything higher than a pole lying on the ground."

"It's no accident!" the doctor shouted. "This is the third time he's escaped. And now those potato farmers are threatening to sue me! I may be arrested!"

"I suppose he jumps, though," Harry said slowly, still working through the situation in his mind. "There's no other way he could get into my paddock. Unless you put him there, that is."

"I haven't seen him since yesterday," the doctor retorted. He took an audible breath, clearly trying to calm himself. "I'm holding you to the bargain we made, Mr. deLeyer. I want you to buy that horse back. Today."

Harry couldn't help smiling. "I'll be right over with a check," he said. "Tell the police and the potato farmers that there will be no more damage to their crops."

He hung up and sat gazing thoughtfully at the telephone. He'd worked with jumping horses all his life, but he'd never met one that had learned to jump by itself. He'd never known one that had jumped for fun. This was very interesting.

After speaking with the doctor, Harry felt certain that the man had had nothing to do with Snowman ending up in Harry's paddock. That meant the big gray horse must have jumped in—even though that paddock was designed to keep jumpers inside the yard.

"Even Wayward Wind couldn't have jumped that fence or gate," he murmured. "Even Sinjon!"

He thought about waking Johanna to tell her what had happened, but quickly decided against it. They were expecting another baby soon, and she needed her sleep. So he tiptoed across the room and back outside, slipping once more into his wooden shoes.

When he reached the paddock, Snowman was still frisking about. But by now he'd added a new part to his game.

The previous afternoon Harry had been working a horse in the paddock. He'd set up a three-foot jump in the center. And now Snowman was galloping toward it!

"Whoa!" Harry exclaimed. The horse was coming at the obstacle at a sharp diagonal angle.

But Snowman didn't hesitate, leaping over the jump out of stride and then galloping on. Harry laughed. Nobody would ever train a jumper to come in at such an angle. But if Snowman had cleared the paddock fence, a sharp angle to a low obstacle was clearly no challenge to his scope!

Harry watched Snowman play for a few more minutes and then realized it was getting late. He had work to do before leaving for the Knox School. Still, his thoughts were on Snowman as he cleaned stalls and measured out feed. He always did his best thinking while engaged in such work.

After he'd filled the last hay manger, he returned to the paddock and whistled to Snowman. The gray gelding trotted over to him, and Harry patted him.

"You want to be a jumper, eh?" he said softly. "Fine. I'll make a jumper out of you."

CHAPTER 8

The Jumper

WHEN HARRY RETURNED TO THE HOUSE, JOHANNA was still in bed. He went in to wake her, knowing she'd want to hear what had happened.

"Anything wrong?" she asked sleepily, blinking up at him.

"Snowman is back." Harry waited a moment for that much to sink in and then added, "He jumped the doctor's fence, and ours too."

"He jumped our fence?" Johanna sat up, startled and now wide-awake.

Harry grinned. "Yes. He trampled some potato plants on his way home. The doctor never wants to see him again."

"So you bought him back." A smile crept across Johanna's face.

"Yes," Harry said. "And I'm going to make a jumper out of him."

Johanna nodded. "There's always been something special about that horse."

Harry shrugged. "He's not a jumper yet," he warned. "He hits the poles at times, and occasionally the standards, too."

"You jumped with him already?" Johanna asked in surprise.

"No. But he was jumping the vertical in the paddock just for fun."

Johanna laughed. "Oh, I wish I'd seen that!" she exclaimed. "It brings me back to you jumping that other plow horse back in North Carolina."

Harry grinned. "That horse did all right. Snowman might too. If he doesn't fall all over himself, that is."

"You don't believe he'll fall all over himself," Johanna chided.

"I guess not," Harry admitted.

"You're already thinking you can make a champion jumper out of him," she said teasingly.

Harry chuckled, but then a faraway look came into his blue eyes. "You never know," he said softly. "From the first time I saw him, I had an odd feeling about that horse."

Johanna nodded and pushed back the covers. "It's time for the children to get up," she said. "You'd better go tell them that Snowman is back to stay."

Chef, Harriet, and Marty greeted the news with whoops of joy. There was a wild scramble to get dressed and out to the paddock. The three children were swarming all over Snowman when Harry and Johanna caught up to them.

"Welcome home, Snowman!" Harriet cried happily, stretching her arms as far as they would go around the big horse's neck.

Chef was perched on the fence, scratching Snowman's head and neck as hard as he could. "I knew you'd be back."

Harry winked at Johanna. "I wish I could stay for the welcome home party," he said. "But I need to drop off a check at the doctor's house on my way to work."

As he hurried off toward the car, he was pretty sure the children hadn't even noticed he was leaving.

If Harry had any lingering doubts about Snowman's jumping abilities, they were gone by the end of the week. The big gray horse's escapades were the talk of the town. The potato farmers and others were more than eager to tell anyone who would listen about seeing Snowman leaping easily over walls and fences.

Before long, visitors started stopping by Hollandia Farm wanting a look at the big gray gelding who jumped fences all on his own. None were very impressed once they got a look at Snowman standing calmly in his stall or dozing in the sun out in the pasture. Most went away at least half convinced that the whole story was a publicity stunt concocted by Harry deLeyer to call attention to Hollandia Farm.

But Harry knew better. He paid little attention to the looky-loos as he began Snowman's jumper training.

In those days there were many methods of training a horse to jump, some of them cruel and unethical. Drugs, electric spurs, other nasty devices—Harry had no use for any of them. They were meant to force a horse to work against his natural inclinations, and Harry didn't want any jumper of his to be trained that way. He had much better luck using firm kindness, gaining the trust of the horse before asking him to learn new things. That wasn't to say that Harry wouldn't discipline a horse that needed it or be tough with a horse that had been spoiled by careless handling. But he always wanted to be fair, to form a partnership with his mount, and he knew that his method was the best way to do that.

In Snowman's case, Harry didn't need to spend any time winning the horse's trust and confidence. He already had those things. Sometimes he thought he'd had them from the moment Snowman had winked at him on that snowy day in Pennsylvania.

Even so, Harry would need plenty of patience for this particular project. Snowman had a lot to learn, but he also had a lot to unlearn. His self-taught approach to jumping was not well suited to jumping a course in the ring, especially a large one. He needed to learn to take off closer to the base of a jump, which would enable him to clear higher and wider jumps.

Harry tried to start teaching him this over small jumps at first. But he soon figured out that small jumps didn't impress Snowman much. He was more apt to knock down the top rail of a three-foot obstacle than one a foot or more higher, which he cleared with ease.

Snowman was a quirky horse, which made him challenging to teach. He wasn't a fast learner, either. But Harry didn't hurry him. He believed in bringing a jumper along slowly rather than rushing him and risking scaring him or burning him out. He spent the rest of that fall and winter honing Snowman's skills and teaching him what he would need to know.

All the while, he imagined what Snowman might do in the show ring someday. He was sure some people would be surprised, even disdainful, to see a horse of his type walk in, but Harry didn't worry much about that. The open jumper divisions of the time were a little different from what they are today. The jumps weren't as varied or the courses as technical, and while the horse's performance was all that counted, he had to do more than just leave the fences standing. There was a whole list of ways to rack up faults on course. Touching a jump with a hind foot was a half fault; touching with a front foot was one fault. Knocking down a pole with the hind feet meant a penalty of two faults, and knocking down a pole with the fronts was four faults. A first refusal—stopping or ducking around a jump—was three faults, and a second refusal called for six faults. The team with the lowest number of faults was the winner.

That meant Snowman had to learn to be accurate and careful over the jumps. He would have to jump not only high and wide, but clean as well. Harry worked on teaching him this, and also on introducing him to the types of jumps he might see in a show. These included coops, which looked like a long A-frame henhouse; brush fences with evergreen branches stuffed in them; and the hog's back—a set of three rails, with the center pole higher than the one in front and in back of it. Some of these jumps were very wide as well as high—sometimes as much as six feet wide. All of them, along with the more ordinary rail and gate jumps, were meant to resemble obstacles a horse might encounter cross-country.

Probably nobody but Harry would have had the patience and persistence to spend hours and days and weeks teaching an easygoing plow horse to become an open jumper. But Harry was up to the task, and Snowman was a good student despite his shortcomings. He had natural balance, good form, and an even pace that looked slower than it was at times. All Harry had to do was teach Snowman that every jump had to be his best.

During this period of training, Chef and Harriet often exercised Snowman when Harry was too busy. Marty, who was growing fast, rode him sometimes as well. The big gray gelding remained kind and easy for the children to handle, seeming to enjoy the attention. After a while Harry also began to rent him out to men who wanted a sure-footed and easy-to-handle foxhunter for a day's outing. That gave Snowman even more practice over varied obstacles and terrain, as well as helping to keep him fit.

Eventually, Harry also let some of the girls from the Knox School enter Snowman in junior shows to give him a feel of the show ring. His performance in those shows was adequate but never spectacular; he won a few ribbons, but he generally collected faults because the low jumps didn't offer enough of a challenge to keep him interested and careful.

Still, Harry was pleased with the big horse's progress, and Snowman seemed pleased with his new life as a jumper-in-training. He worked hard, cleaned up his food eagerly, and looked better every day—sleek and muscular. He was as calm and reliable as ever, but showed a new zest for life, a livelier spirit that told Harry he was happy.

Harry's life was changing too. Little William deLeyer had been born by then, and his older siblings were joking about how soon he would be allowed to ride Snowman.

One day Johanna brought the baby out to watch Harry working Snowman in the ring. The baby was half asleep, but Johanna watched with interest as her husband put Snowman over a line of good-sized jumps. When Harry rode closer, she couldn't help commenting on the way he'd loosened the reins a few strides before each jump. Harry nodded and gave Snowman a pat.

"I know my method might raise eyebrows among some of the jumper trainers around here," he told his wife with a smile. "But I think it helps give a horse self-confidence. I want him to feel that he is responsible for the jump. Oh, I'm still there, guiding him with my legs and voice, but not controlling Snowman's every move."

The big gray pricked his ears at the sound of his name, and baby William gurgled and laughed as the horse stretched over the fence to sniff at him.

Harry smiled again. "Come on, Snowman," he said, picking up the reins. "Let's try it again." He gestured toward Chef and Harriet, who were standing in the ring. "Let's put it up another hole!"

The children hurried to do as he said, then stood back to watch. "Snowman hardly ever touches a rail anymore," Harriet commented.

Chef nodded. "Do you think Dad will enter him in a real show soon?"

"I hope so." Harriet watched Snowman sail easily over the higher jump. "But he'd better hurry. Spring is almost over already!"

"I know." Chef sighed, knowing it was true. The 1958 show season was already in full swing, with shows every weekend. "If he doesn't hurry, Snowman will never be able to catch up in the points and become the year-end champion!"

Harriet held her breath as Snowman jumped the next obstacle. Then she let it out again and looked at her brother. "Do you think we should ask him?"

Chef shrugged and chewed his lip. "No point doing that. I suppose he'll tell us when he's ready."

CHAPTER 9

Sands Point, 1958

"SANDS POINT," HARRY ANNOUNCED TO HIS FAMILY over dinner one evening. "That's the one."

"What?" Johanna said.

But Chef caught on right away. "You mean Snowman?" he cried. "That's great!"

Harriet and Marty cheered too, and the baby banged his spoon on the tray of his high chair. Harry smiled at his wife. Snowman had recently competed in his first show, a tiny local one at Rice Farms. He'd won a jumper class there, clearing every fence with ease. But Harry knew the big gray was destined for more than local ribbons.

"Sands Point. Yes, that's the show I've decided on as a real test for Snowman," he said.

"Wonderful," Johanna replied. "That's quite a tough show, though, isn't it?"

Harry nodded. He'd thought of that, too. The Sands Point show was known for its rugged, challenging jumper courses. Only a really good horse had a chance of winning there. But that was why Harry had chosen it. If Snowman performed well at Sands Point, it would prove that he had what it took to be an open jumper.

In those days, Harry wasn't really part of the horse elite of the area. Oh, he was known to most of the professional horse trainers, of course. No rider as good as he was could remain anonymous for long. But he wasn't among the exclusive group that entered all the big-time shows on the circuit.

He did have friends among that group, however. One of them was Dave Kelly, who rode a difficult but talented mare named Andante. Andante had been the Professional Horsemen's Association horse of the year not once, but twice. She was expected to win the championship at Sands Point, one of the bigger shows on the eastern circuit, just as she'd done the previous two years running.

Harry and Snowman weren't the only ones willing to take on the great mare in the Sands Point open jumper competition, however. Twenty horses were entered, including several great champions of the day—Saxon Wood, Bellaire, Red Lantern, and others. When Harry looked over the entry list, he saw that Snowman would be the least-experienced competitor by far. That was no surprise, and it might have made another man nervous. But Harry had confidence in Snowman, and he looked forward to proving what the big gray horse could do among such elite company.

The morning of the show started very early for the deLeyer clan. Baby William was left in the care of a neighbor woman for the day. Johanna and the three older children clopped around the stable in their wooden shoes, helping Harry and his two grooms clean the stables, feed the horses, and load the tack and other equipment Harry would need for the three days of the show.

Finally, it was time to load the horses for the drive to the showgrounds. Snowman wasn't the only Hollandia horse who would be competing at Sands Point. Harry had entered Wayward Wind in the first-year green hunters, and a young gelding named Cicero in the second-year green hunters. He would also be riding a mare known as Night Arrest, owned by one of the Knox School students he taught. Night Arrest was a wild little mare with a nervous body and a head full of crazy ideas. She'd come to her owner with plenty of bad habits, which Harry was doing his best to train out of her. In the meantime, he didn't trust the mare enough to allow anyone but himself to ride her.

Snowman walked into the trailer as calmly as ever. Chef watched, dancing from one foot to the other from the excitement of the big day.

"Snowman looks ready to go!" he exclaimed.

Harriet nodded. "He already knows that a trailer ride always means jumping," she said. "I bet he can't wait!"

"I wish I could be as calm as he is," their mother quipped.

"Me too." Chef shivered with anticipation. "I hope Andante gets lost on the way to the show."

"Or Dave gets sick," Harriet added hopefully.

"No danger of either happening," Harry told them with a smile.

Johanna grabbed the capering Chef by the shoulder and steered him toward the house. "Go change into your good clothes," she ordered. "We'll be leaving soon."

The children rushed into the house to change while Harry and the grooms loaded the other horses. By the time they returned, it was time to go.

The showgrounds were busy when the deLeyers arrived. There were a thousand horses entered in the show, and spectators had come from all around to watch some of the stars of the sport compete. Men, women, and children crowded the bleachers, stood at the fence of the show rings, or watched from their cars in the tailgating area. The whole place had a festive atmosphere, and the deLeyer children hardly knew where to look first.

"When will Snowman compete?" Chef asked as the grooms lead the horses off the trailer.

"Not until later," Harry told him. "Hunters come first, then jumpers after that."

Hunters and jumpers were both competitions involving horses jumping fences in the show ring, but they were very different. The hunter horses had to be elegant and beautiful, with flawless gaits and perfect jumping forms. The jumpers, like Snowman, merely had to get over the jumps with as few faults as possible. There was no way Snowman could have been competitive as a hunter; in those days, only Thoroughbreds were considered suitable for the division. But as a jumper, it was his performance that would count, not his breeding, looks, or way of moving.

The children and Johanna hurried off to watch Harry's first ride, which was on Wayward Wind in the first-year green hunters. The highest jumps were three foot six inches, an easy height for the talented mare. Harry was already convinced that Wayward Wind would make it as an open jumper, but he was taking things slowly, getting her used to showing over the smaller jumps in the hunter ring. Besides that, she was a beautiful horse with superb form. The judges at Sands Point seemed to think so too. When the division was over, Wayward Wind was the winner.

"Thank you," Harry said with a smile as the ringmaster pinned the ribbon on the mare's bridle. Then he lifted a hand to acknowledge the polite applause from the crowd.

Next came the second-year green hunters. Harry rode Cicero, who had competed in the division before. Once again, Harry ended up with a blue ribbon. This time the applause was a little louder and lasted a little longer. Only some of the spectators had known the name Harry deLeyer before this, but many were starting to take notice of him now.

Then Harry went on to win the green jumper stake and the green jumper championship on his student's horse, Night Arrest. People all over the showgrounds started thumbing through their programs and asking the people around them about Harry. Word spread that he taught riding at the Knox School and owned a small stable known as Hollandia Farm.

"Well done, sir!" someone in the crowd called as Harry rode past after accepting Night Arrest's ribbons.

Harry tipped his hat and smiled in response. But his mind had already moved on to his next ride: Snowman.

CHAPTER 10

Open Jumpers: Day One

CHEF AND HARRIET WERE TENSE AS THE OPEN JUMP-
ers paraded into the ring so the crowd could have a look.
"There's Snowman!" Harriet cried, pointing so excitedly
that she almost fell off her perch. Johanna had gone to sit
in the bleachers, but the children were allowed to sit on the
ring fence for a closer view of the action. Dozens of other
children and teenagers had joined them there.

Chef just nodded, his eyes never leaving the big gray.

But his sister was surveying the competition. "That
bay horse looks ready to explode," she observed as a rider
wrestled with his fiery mount.

Most of the horses were keyed up, dancing and tossing
their heads as they high-stepped through the gate into the
ring. Except for Snowman, all of them were Thoroughbreds
or similar sport-bred types, aristocratic and lean.

"Check out that flea-bitten gray," someone exclaimed with a laugh from the bleachers behind the deLeyer children. "Did he accidentally wander off the farm and into the show?"

Chef turned to glare at the man who had spoken, but in the crowd of spectators, couldn't tell who had made the comment. Almost everyone was staring at Snowman, many of them laughing or looking surprised.

The big-boned gray gelding did present a remarkable sight, ambling along on a loose rein among the willowy, energetic jumpers. But most of the crowd recognized Harry by now and knew this was no joke. Harry deLeyer was going to ride this comical-looking horse in the open jumpers!

"Poor Snowman," Harriet muttered as she heard someone else laugh.

But Chef grinned. "Don't feel sorry for Snowman," he told his sister. "He loves all the attention. Look!"

Sure enough, Snowman almost seemed to be smiling as he turned his head toward the crowd, pricking his ears in a friendly and alert way. A little girl perched next to Chef let out a gasp.

"Hey," she cried. "That funny old horse just winked at me!"

Chef glanced at her disdainfully. "Sure he did," he said with a sniff.

More and more spectators were crowding forward for a

look at Snowman. In the tailgating area, people set down their drinks and stood atop Jaguars and Thunderbirds for a better view of the big gray plow horse.

"How funny!" a woman exclaimed somewhere in the bleachers behind where the deLeyer children were sitting. "Can that broad-beamed old thing even jump?"

"It's an insult to the others, that's what it is," a man put in, sounding irritated. "How can a horse like that stand in the same ring with Andante? Especially this year, when she's out to retire the trophy!"

Harriet leaned closer to her brother. "What's 'retire the trophy' mean?" she whispered.

"If Andante wins this year, it'll be her third time," Chef replied. "She'd get to keep the trophy."

"Oh." Harriet turned and glared in the general direction of the commenter, though she wasn't certain where he was. "Well, she won't have to worry about that, because Snowman's going to win!"

Chef just nodded and crossed his fingers. He hoped his sister was right.

The horses were leaving the ring by now. Snowman was still moving along calmly, his head high as he continued looking around. The spectators watched until he was out of sight and then turned their attention to the first competitor.

Most in the crowd were horse enthusiasts, and the spectacle of the big gray horse didn't hold their interest for long once the action started. There were oohs and aahs and sighs of sympathy as the horses entered the ring one by one to take their turns over the tough jumper course. As expected, Andante took an early lead, though the contest wouldn't be decided until the end of the third day. Some of the other horses didn't do as well, refusing some of the jumps or dumping a rider.

When Snowman's turn came, once again, the crowd watched with interest. There were a few chuckles when he picked up the canter to begin his course; clearly some were expecting the big gray to plow into the first fence and go down amid flying poles. But the laughter faded away when Snowman cleared the first obstacle effortlessly, then the next. He had a few faults here and there, mostly on the lower jumps on the course, but Harry was smiling when they pulled up at the end of the round. Yes, that would do for a start.

CHAPTER 11

Open Jumpers: Day Two

ON THE SECOND DAY OF THE OPEN JUMPER COMPETI- tion, things went much the same, at least at first. Andante performed brilliantly, giving the other competitors a mark to shoot for. She was still holding a narrow lead when Snowman's turn came.

"Go, Snowman, go," Harriet whispered. She and her brothers were back in their spots on the rail.

"He can do it." Chef clutched the wooden fence so tightly his knuckles were white.

"Yay, Snowman!" little Marty cried so loudly that the people nearby laughed and craned their heads to see who had shouted.

Then the big gray picked up a canter, and all eyes were on the action in the ring once again. Harry felt focused and calm as he circled Snowman at one end. Yesterday's competition had showed him that he would have to ride Snowman accurately and firmly, especially over the easier obstacles, which the big horse was prone to take less seriously than the more challenging ones.

They turned and headed for the first obstacle at a strong but steady hand gallop. Snowman pricked his ears at the fence and then cleared it cleanly and hand galloped on. The second fence went just as well, and the third . . .

Harry rode carefully, making sure the big gray knew exactly what he wanted at each obstacle. Snowman responded just as Harry had hoped, putting in the effort needed to sail over each jump without so much as a hoof touching a rail.

By the time they approached the final fence, a wide brush-and-rail jump, the crowd was holding its collective breath. Everyone in the place knew that Andante's lead was slim. If this funny-looking gray horse jumped a clean round, the two would be tied going into the final day's competition!

"Okay, Snowman," Harry murmured as the obstacle neared. Three strides, two strides, one . . .

The gray horse's powerful hindquarters thrust up and forward, his forelegs lifted, and Harry leaned forward, letting the reins go slack to allow his mount the full use of his head and neck.

Snowman tucked his front hooves and arced cleanly over

the ragged topline of the brush fence. But on the landing, one hind leg came forward a little too far, and the iron shoe on that hoof ripped down through the flesh of the foreleg already on the ground. It was a miscalculation of inches, but one that could spell disaster.

Harry could feel right away that something was wrong, though nobody in the crowd seemed to notice as applause rose for Snowman's round and everyone started chattering excitedly about what this meant. Tomorrow, this ungainly farm horse would be going head-to-head with the great Andante for the championship! For his part, Snowman never missed a stride as he cantered off toward the exit gate.

Johanna was there to meet him. "His leg," she said to Harry. "I saw what happened. Is he all right?"

"I don't know." Harry urged the horse forward, wanting to get him away from the crowds as quickly as possible. "We'll check him back at the stall."

Meanwhile, Chef was peering toward his parents and Snowman, who were now rapidly disappearing behind the crowd. Chef gripped his sister's hand. "Snowman!" he gasped out. "His foreleg is bleeding!"

Harriet let out a cry of dismay and then leaped down from the fence. She and Chef raced toward the stabling area with Marty on their heels.

Harry jumped down from the saddle as soon as they'd

reached the relative quiet of the stabling area. The children came panting up at the same time, out of breath and with their blue eyes shining with anxiety.

The wound looked bad. It was bleeding now in earnest, and Harry winced.

"Oh, Snowman," Harriet exclaimed. "I thought you were over being clumsy!"

"It's not his fault," Chef chided her. Biting his lip, he glanced at Harry. "That wound'll stiffen and swell overnight, won't it?"

"Does this mean he's out of tomorrow's show?" Johanna put in. Without waiting for an answer, she shook her head. "And just when he was about to be champion!"

Harry didn't respond for a moment, squatting down and probing the wound gently with his fingers. There was no sign of bone splinters, and nothing seemed to be fractured. If the wound had been a little deeper, Snowman's jumping career might have been over almost before it had started. That didn't seem to be the case, which was a relief. But Harry knew that Chef was right—the leg would be badly swollen by morning. Still thinking hard, he turned to unbuckle the girth on Snowman's saddle.

"We're not licked yet," he told the family.

"You can try to bandage it," Harriet said hopefully.

"It's too late for that," Harry replied.

"You'd better get a vet," Chef suggested.

Marty had been staring at Snowman's wound with huge, worried eyes. Now, he moved closer, wrapping his arms around the horse's other front leg. Tears squeezed out of his eyes as he looked up at the gray head above him.

"It hurts," Marty said in a whisper. "It hurts."

Snowman lowered his head as though to assure the little boy that there was nothing to worry about. Then he turned to look at Harry, seeming to include him in that assurance.

Harry smiled at the horse and gave him a pat. Then he glanced at his family. "It's going to be a long night for me," he said.

"What do you mean?" Chef asked. "What are you going to do?"

"Clean up the wound and fix an ice pack," Harry told him. "I'll keep it filled all night."

"I'll help you," Chef said at once. "I don't mind staying awake."

Harry patted his son on the shoulder. "Thanks." He glanced at Johanna. "You might as well take the others back to the hotel."

Harriet tried to protest, but Johanna herded her and Marty away, leaving Harry and Chef to fuss over Snowman. Luckily, the grooms were there to look after the other horses, though they kept glancing in at the big gray gelding every time they passed. There was little talk around the Hollandia

Farm show stalls, though. Everyone there was almost as concerned about Snowman as Harry himself.

With Chef assisting him, Harry washed and disinfected the wound. Then the two of them rubbed Snowman down and covered him with a sheet, making him comfortable in his stall.

"Now," Harry said, brushing off his hands and looked around. "We'll need to find some materials to make an ice pack."

Leaving the grooms to keep an eye on Snowman and the others, he and Chef hopped into the station wagon. Harry had noticed a gas station near the showgrounds that he thought might have what he needed.

At the station, Harry bought a discarded inner tube. "What do you need this for?" the clerk asked as he handed it over. "The boy's bike break down?"

Harry merely smiled. "Do you sell ice here?" he asked.

The clerk pointed toward an ice machine. Harry was pleased. The station was open all night; he would be able to return for more ice whenever he needed it.

Soon, he and Chef had filled up several large sacks with ice cubes. Then they drove back to the showgrounds. When they arrived, Harry cut the inner tube to the right length to slip over Snowman's leg. He tied it tightly at the bottom and then filled the tube with ice almost to the top. The final step was lashing it securely to the leg to keep it in place.

"Do you think that'll work?" Chef asked, eyeing his father's odd-looking ice boot.

Harry shrugged. "He'll be all right for a while," he said. "Let's go grab some dinner."

That evening's meal was a somber affair. "William all right?" Harry asked Johanna as he poked his fork into his food.

She nodded. "I called home just now," she said. "He's full of milk, and asleep."

Harry smiled briefly and then took a bite, which he chewed for a very long time. Nobody seemed to have much of an appetite except for Marty, who had two helpings of meat and potatoes.

Johanna was afraid to say much. She was sure that Snowman would be too stiff and sore to compete tomorrow. But she didn't want to voice the thought out loud— she could tell that Harry hadn't given up yet. Still . . .

When Harry pushed his chair back from the table, Chef sat up straight. "Can I go back to the stalls with you?"

Harry shook his head. "You have to get to bed."

"I told you, I don't mind staying awake," Chef argued. "Can't I at least stay up until ten?"

Harry smiled. "Until ten," he agreed.

When they reached Snowman's stall, the big gray was standing calmly. His big head swung over the half door in greeting. His ears were cocked forward, and his eyes held their usual bright gleam.

Harry patted him. "You big teddy bear," he said fondly, using his favorite nickname for Snowman. "You're going to beat Andante tomorrow, aren't you?"

"He sure is!" Chef said.

Harry checked the ice in the pack. It had melted quite a bit, so he and Chef replaced it with fresh ice. Then they sat down on campstools just outside the stall. Both of them were tired, and there wasn't much talking; in fact, both father and son dozed off after a while. But at five minutes to ten, Harry nudged Chef awake.

"Time to be off to bed," he said.

Chef yawned and climbed to his feet. Snowman stood at the stall door looking out at them.

"Good night, you big lug," Chef told the horse.

Once Chef was gone, Harry refilled the ice pack again. After he finished, he stood gazing at Snowman.

"No faults tomorrow," he said softly. "You can beat Andante—but only if you watch your big feet on the lower jumps."

Snowman stepped to the door and nuzzled Harry. Harry dug his fingers into the coarse hair of the gray's neck, and Snowman responded with his usual grimace.

Then the horse turned away to nose at the hay the grooms had left in his stall, and Harry returned to his stool. He sat down and yawned, leaning back against the wall. It was late, and it had been a long day. He listened to the night sounds of horses, crickets, and the distant song of a frog-pond chorus until he dozed off.

But he didn't sleep for long. Every hour or so, for the rest of the night, Harry rose and went to replenish the ice packed around Snowman's injured leg. Sometime after midnight he returned to the gas station for a fresh supply. He knew that sitting up most of the night would do his nerves and reflexes little good. But the best ride in the world wouldn't matter if he didn't keep Snowman's leg from swelling and getting stiff. So he climbed to his feet time after time, talking to Snowman as he worked, reminding him how they would have to be at their best to beat Andante and the others.

Finally, sometime before dawn, Harry finished tending the ice pack and sat down again. This time the little stool seemed too hard and uncomfortable, so he slipped to the ground, sitting with his back against the stall door. Snowman lowered his head so that his muzzle rested close to Harry's shoulder. Man and horse relaxed, and Harry quickly dropped off to sleep—a real sleep this time, deep and restful.

CHAPTER 12

The Final Day

HARRY JERKED AWAKE SUDDENLY, LEAPING TO HIS feet almost before his eyes were open. He staggered slightly, catching himself on the stall door and looking around with alarm. It was broad daylight, which meant it was hours later than he usually awakened at a show.

He rubbed his eyes and checked his watch. Nearly six o'clock. Snowman was awake, watching him calmly.

"Good morning," Harry mumbled, rubbing the horse's big gray nose.

He looked around. Night Arrest and Wayward Wind weren't in their stalls, and Harry guessed that the grooms had taken them out to stretch their legs.

Snowman let out a nicker. It was past the time he normally got his morning oats. But that could wait a moment longer.

Swallowing hard, Harry opened the stall door and stepped

inside. The tube on Snowman's wounded leg was limp and deflated; the ice must have melted hours ago. Still, the horse appeared to be putting equal weight on both forelegs.

"Did you stay on your feet all night?" Harry murmured, giving the gray a rub on the neck. Harry guessed that the ice pack had felt too awkward for Snowman to be comfortable lying down. Horses could sleep standing up, but Harry wished the big gray had had a chance to take the weight off his injured leg.

He kneeled down, putting a hand on the ice pack. He hesitated for a moment before reaching for the ties holding the tube in place. His fingers fumbled with the knots, but finally, he got them loose. Slowly, carefully, he slid the tube off Snowman's leg.

At that moment he sensed rather than heard someone behind him. Turning his head, he saw Johanna standing in the open stall doorway. Her hair was in disarray, and her hazel eyes were worried; Harry guessed that she'd rushed over as soon as she'd awakened.

She leaned past Harry for a look at the leg. "No swelling!" she exclaimed softly.

Harry smiled at her. "Not a trace."

"What a relief!"

"Yes." Harry stood up. "But the real test is yet to come." He took hold of Snowman's mane, pulling gently. "Come with me, Snowman."

The big horse followed along willingly as Harry led him out of the stall and across the street to a training paddock. He walked without a limp, though Harry tried not to get too excited.

The paddock was empty except for a practice jump set up in the center. Swinging open the gate, Harry released the horse inside. Snowman leaped into motion immediately, cantering around the ring eagerly.

Leaving his wife at the gate, Harry jogged toward the jump in the middle. Snowman saw where he was heading and swung around toward him. Cantering straight to the obstacle, he sailed over it.

Several passing grooms paused to watch, surprised to see a riderless horse taking a jump. Johanna laughed at the expressions on their faces and then let herself into the ring. Racing over to Harry, she flung her arms around him.

"You've worked a miracle!" she cried, her Dutch accent coming out more strongly as it always did when she was excited.

Harry laughed. "The ice worked a miracle," he said, his eyes twinkling.

He knew that this didn't mean that Snowman was as good as new. His sore leg might still give out on him once he tackled the tough jumps in the show ring.

But at least they still had a chance.

• • •

"Is he okay?" Chef asked as Johanna walked toward the Hollandia show stalls with Snowman strolling along beside her on a lead rope. Chef and Johanna had been keeping the big gray horse moving all morning, wanting to make sure his wounded leg stayed limber.

"He's fine!" Marty danced forward from his mother's side. "He's still okay!"

"Good," Harriet said with relief. "Because everyone is talking about him."

"Yeah! Everyone expects a real duel today between Snowman and Andante." Chef's expression darkened. "But lots of people say there's no way an old plow horse can beat a well-bred show champion."

Harry hurried over just in time to hear him. "Never mind that," he said. "It's no real surprise that most of the horsemen around here still favor Andante. She's a known quantity."

"Hmph," Chef said, not looking convinced.

"Time to get tacked up and start warming up," Harry told Snowman with a pat.

"We'll help!" Harriet cried, and she and her brothers scampered off to grab the saddle and bridle.

Harry was red-eyed and weary as he swung into the saddle a few minutes later. He held his breath, still not fully daring to believe that Snowman was really all right until he felt the horse trot off soundly beneath him.

Soon after that, the third and final day of the open jumper competition began. As Harry and Snowman waited their turn, they kept track of how the others were doing. There wasn't much chance that any other team could beat Snowman and Andante, who were well ahead in points. But anything could happen with horses, and so, Harry did his best to pay attention, though he was still tired and not feeling his best.

When Andante's turn came, the beautiful mare pranced in through the gate, looking fit and ready to go. She leaped forward as soon as Dave Kelly gave the cue, speeding toward the first jump, a brush-and-rail. Andante cleared it with room to spare, then landed and galloped on toward the hogsback obstacle, followed by an imposing wall jump.

Every jump was better than the last. By the time she landed over the final fence, the crowd was already applauding. The mare tossed her head as she left the ring, seeming to know she'd done well.

"There you go," Harry told Snowman with a rub on the withers. "The horse to beat."

A few minutes later it was Snowman's turn. When he trotted in through the gate, the only applause came from the children lined up on the rail.

"Go, Snowman!" a little girl cried.

Sitting among Snowman's cheering young fans, Chef and Harriet traded a smile. "At least somebody believes in Snowman besides us," Harriet whispered.

"Right." Chef grinned. "They can tell he likes kids."

Harry barely heard the cheers as he sent Snowman into a canter and aimed him toward the first jump. The big gray pricked his ears eagerly, swinging along with even strides.

"Let's go, Snowman," Harry whispered as he leaned forward to meet the jump.

Snowman sailed up and over the brush-and-rail, tucking his feet up carefully. Next came the hog's back—four foot nine inches high with a five-foot spread. Harry measured the distance with his eyes, being careful to get Snowman to the jump at just the right pace for takeoff. Up and over!

As they landed, Harry turned the gelding's head slightly to take some of the strain off the injured leg as they made a sharp turn to the wall. Snowman didn't falter, galloping on strongly and leaping easily over the wall. Another turn, and they were up and over a tall triple bar.

Harry's heart pounded in time with the horse's big hooves. He couldn't detect a single move, not the tiniest hesitation to indicate that Snowman might be favoring his right foreleg. Snowman cleared one jump and then another, and before Harry quite realized it, only one obstacle remained—a five-foot high brush-and-rail.

The round had been clean so far. Unlike Andante, who had skimmed over many of the jumps with little room to spare, Snowman was jumping high and wide, leaving plenty of daylight over each jump. If he went clean over the last one, he would beat Andante's score and win the open jumper championship.

The big gray horse galloped across the ring toward the final brush-and-rail. The jump looked enormous, but Harry knew that was the way Snowman liked them. The horse's ears were pricked, and Harry imagined him laughing as he took off, his powerful hind legs thrusting him up and over in a clean, graceful arc of gray horseflesh.

After they landed, there was a long moment of silence. The children were the first to shout out, and the rest of the crowd soon joined in, cheering and whistling and applauding like mad. Snowman had won them over at last! He was a real-life Cinderella story, right here in front of them in a ring of jumps on Long Island, New York.

"Come on!" Chef shouted, leaping down from the fence.

Harriet was hot on his heels in a wild race to meet Snowman at the stalls. Marty did his best to keep up, though his short legs were no match for their excitement.

"Wait . . . for . . . meee!" he wailed as he ran in their wake.

Johanna and the older children reached the stall just as Harry swung the saddle off the big gray's back. He was talking to him as he worked.

"I told you that you could do it," he was saying when Johanna reached his side. He glanced at her sheepishly, wondering what she would think of him talking to Snowman as if he were a person.

But Johanna hardly noticed. "He was wonderful!" she exclaimed, rubbing Snowman's muzzle. "Our champion!"

"You big hero!" Harriet shouted, flinging her arms around Snowman's chest.

"He's the champ," Chef agreed, his grin stretching from ear to ear. "Nobody can beat him."

Marty finally arrived, huffing and puffing and red-faced with exertion and annoyance. He sputtered accusingly at Chef and Harriet, who ignored him, then shrugged and hugged one of Snowman's legs.

Harry finished untacking the big horse and then clipped a lead rope to his halter. Snowman would need to be walked until he'd cooled down from all the exertion.

"We'll walk him and rub him down," Chef offered.

Harry smiled with relief and turned over the lead rope without a word. Harriet started walking while Chef rushed off to fetch a cooler. Harry was glad to let them do it. It had been a big day—a big three days!—and he could use a rest.

CHAPTER 13

Decisions

A FEW DAYS AFTER THE SANDS POINT SHOW, JOHANNA was mending a shirt in the living room when Harry walked in. She could tell right away that he had something on his mind.

He offered her the bottle of soda he was holding. "I'd like a glass, too," she said as she accepted it.

Harry smiled. "I forgot that you don't like to drink out of a bottle." He hurried off, returning moments later with a glass, and a soda for himself. Then he sat down beside his wife.

Johanna didn't ask what he wanted. She knew he would tell her when he was ready. Although she had a good idea what the topic might be . . .

Harry took a deep drink of his soda. "About Snowman," he began, and then hesitated.

"He could be a national champion," Johanna said with a smile.

"I think so," Harry said eagerly. "He has the heart, the strength."

He'd been thinking about Snowman a lot these past few days. He was certain that the big gray gelding had the potential to be a national champion as Johanna had said. But giving him that chance would mean hitting the horse show circuit in earnest. That involved trailering to a new show each weekend—Westport, Lakeville, Branchville, Smithtown, Stony Brook, Piping Rock, Paramus, Harrisburg, Washington. There would be big entry fees, travel expenses, days of riding his heart out with no guarantee of success.

Harry had never been a gambler. Until now, he'd always done the safe, sure thing. Every horse had to earn its keep; every sale had to provide at least some profit.

But now there was Snowman. What was Harry to do with him? After his performance at Sands Point, it would be easy to find a buyer—easy to make that necessary profit on the sale. But something held him back. This wasn't Cicero he was talking about; it wasn't Wayward Wind. He'd always been able to consider them, and countless others, as just part of the business. But Snowman was different. Maybe it was worth the risk. . . .

But he couldn't make the decision alone. He knew what the children would say. They would be all for giving Snowman his chance at that championship, eager to hit the circuit. To them, it would be one big adventure after another, at least until school started up again in the fall.

But he hadn't been sure what Johanna would say. Would she be up for the adventure too? Or would her thrifty Dutch nature win out?

Taking another sip of soda, he looked at her out of the corner of his eye. She was still smiling as she gazed at the bubbles drifting upward in her glass.

"Madison Square Garden," she said dreamily.

Harry grinned. He'd been doing a lot of dreaming himself since Sands Point. Now, with just those three words, he knew that Johanna was on board—that he'd have a chance to try to make those dreams come true. Madison Square Garden in nearby New York City was the site of the National Horse Show, the last big show of the season, and the most prestigious. That was where the important national championships were won and awarded.

"It will mean a long, hard summer and fall," he warned. "I can't ask you and the children to rough it with me."

She gave him an impish grin. "And you can't keep us from being with you as much as we can manage."

As solid and stubborn as he was, Harry never could resist Johanna's smile. He laughed and nodded, not bothering to protest further. It would be nice to have Johanna and the children with him. After all, going to a show had always been a family project, just like running the stable.

"Snowman has to have his chance," Johanna said, setting her glass on the table firmly.

"I feel the same way," Harry said.

Then he jumped to his feet. Now that the decision had been made, he had a lot of work to do.

The next few weeks passed in a blur of hard work and long days. One of the first things Harry had to do was prepare Hollandia Farm to keep running without him being there much of the time. That meant hiring more help, especially since he would be taking the two grooms he already had on the road with him. At the same time, he continued to work with Snowman, honing the big gray's skills even more. He was so busy that he didn't even consider seeing a doctor about a sore spot that had developed on his tongue. He'd had sores and cuts before, and they'd always healed with time and home remedies, so he didn't worry about it.

Snowman's next outing would be the Fairfield County Hunt Club Show in Westport, Connecticut. The four-day show would be a tough test for the big gray, and an important one. A poor showing could put an end to this whole quest, or at least dampen the odds of success. But a good showing would add plenty of points to Snowman's record on top of the ones he'd earned at Sands Point, which would help him catch up in the standings. That was important, since many of the top jumpers had already piled up points toward the year-end championships in earlier shows.

Doing well at Fairfield might even impress the elite circle of horsemen in the area, convince them that a plow horse with unconventional conformation and not a drop of true blue blood could be a champion . . . though Harry didn't care about that. His sole concern was for Snowman.

He studied the competition Snowman would face at the big show. By the time they left for Connecticut, Chef and Harriet could recite the records of most of the jumpers entered. Most imposing were the two big stars of Oak Ridge Stables—First Chance and Sonoro. They'd entered four shows already that spring and had won championships and reserve at all of them. Most horsemen expected the pair to take top honors at Fairfield as well.

The open jumpers didn't start until the second day of the show, which gave Snowman a chance to settle in. Meanwhile, Harry rode his student's tough little mare, Night Arrest, in the first day's green jumper class. She was still far too much of a handful for her owner to ride in a show, and so Harry had agreed to compete her again. She gave him a workout—he had to check and control her in front of every jump—but they ended up second in the division.

That night Harry went to bed early to the sound of rain pounding on the roof. Johanna looked out the window.

"It's really pouring out there," she said. "I hope the course won't be too muddy tomorrow."

Harry heard the note of worry in her voice. He felt it, too. Snowman had never jumped in the mud, and Harry had no way of knowing how he might handle it. The gray gelding had big feet and had once been very clumsy at handling them. Would he slip and slide around the course, taking down rails as he went?

"We'll see," he told his wife. Then he turned over and did his best to fall asleep.

CHAPTER 14
Fairfield

FOR THE FAIRFIELD SHOW, HARRY HAD DECIDED TO try Snowman in a different kind of jumper event. This one was called "the knock down and out." All the horses would jump a course, and any who knocked down even a single rail were eliminated. Whichever horses were left after the first round would move on to a jump-off, with the fences set higher. Snowman's main competition in the class would once again be Andante, with Dave Kelly aboard.

The previous night's heavy rain had left the ring a soggy mess. The horses' hooves splashed with each step they took, and a few of them had trouble negotiating the sloppy footing.

But Harry let out a breath of relief the first time he asked Snowman to trot during their warm-up. The big gray trotted out confidently, planting his big hooves carefully with each stride. When they jumped a small warm-up fence, Snowman was a little slower off the ground than usual, but only because he was being cautious about setting his feet before takeoff.

"Who would have guessed you were such a mudder?" Harry joked with a pat on the neck, using the old racetrack jargon for a horse who liked running on a wet track.

Sure enough, Snowman had little trouble with the course, clearing all the jumps easily. Eleven other horses also went clean, including Andante.

But when the jumps were raised for the jump-off, things changed. Most of the horses had at least one rail down. In the end the only clear rounds the second time around were Andante and Snowman.

That meant there would be another jump-off to determine the winner. The jump crew scurried in to raise the rails again. Dave Kelly was circling Andante nearby; the elegant mare still looked fresh and ready.

Harry waited at the gate with Snowman. "High and wide," he murmured to the big gray, reaching down to rub his neck. "You'll need to go way up this time. Use that old power, Teddy Bear."

Snowman cocked an ear back, seeming to listen carefully to Harry's words. Harry smiled and then glanced over at Andante. He was pretty confident that Snowman could go clean over the new height. But he wouldn't be surprised if Andante did too. She was in fine form, and Dave Kelly was a superb rider. If both horses went clean again, a third jump-off would favor Andante, since the rules stated that time would count in that one, and she was a fast horse.

He gazed down at the solid gray neck in front of him, thinking ahead to the next day, when Snowman would face a field of tough rivals in the open jumper competition. Would he have enough energy left if he went four rounds today?

Soon, the course was ready, and Andante pranced in for her round. She settled down as soon as Dave aimed her at the first fence, and attacked it in her usual professional manner. Harry watched the mare's round carefully, waiting for the telltale clank of hoof on wood, the thump of a rail hitting the ground. But it never came. The crowd cheered as she pulled up—clean again. If Snowman went clean this time as well, there would be a fourth round.

Harry rode in when Snowman's turn was called, trotted halfway around an opening circle and then sent Snowman into a canter. They swung toward the first jump—but after a stride or two, Harry nudged the horse with a knee, sending him off toward a different jump instead.

The crowd muttered, and a few people shouted warnings about going off course, which would mean elimination. But it wasn't a mistake. Harry had decided to let Andante win by default to avoid that third jump-off, which might

Snowman loved to go swimming in the Long Island Sound.

No fence was too high for Snowman.

Devon Horse Show is the oldest and largest outdoor multibreed competition in the United States. In 1961 Harry and Snowman took the grounds by storm.

Snowman may have been a champion show jumper,
but to the deLeyers he was part of the family.

Snowman broke the high jump record by clearing 7'2".

tire Snowman enough to hurt his performance in the open jumpers. He would sacrifice two points by settling for second place in the knock-down-and-out class, but that was all right. He would make up for it tomorrow.

As soon as they cleared the wrong jump, the judge blew a whistle to signal the pair's elimination, and Harry pulled his horse to a walk. Snowman shook his head and snorted, his ears back. It was as close to angry disobedience as he ever came. He'd been ready to jump those high fences, and he wanted to make sure that Harry—and everyone else— knew it.

Harry patted his neck. "Sorry, Teddy Bear," he said. "You'll get your chance at the tough jumps tomorrow."

Back at the stalls, Johanna understood what Harry had done without needing any explanation. But Chef and Harriet were brokenhearted. Their Snowman had been defeated by Andante—without even a fair chance to beat her!

"Oh, Snowman," Harriet chided the big horse as she brushed the sweat marks from his side. "I know you didn't meant to jump the wrong jump. You just have to be more careful, all right?"

Harry, who was working on the horse's other side, peered around at her with a twinkle in his eyes. "Don't worry, I'm sure he won't do it again."

"He'd better not tomorrow," Chef muttered, casting his father a slightly suspicious look.

"Naughty Snowman went the wrong way!" Marty said, lifting a leather strap to spank the horse.

But Chef grabbed the strap before it touched Snowman. "You never hit a horse," he scolded his little brother. "Riders who use a whip make their jumpers knock down poles."

Harry traded a smile with Johanna over the children's heads. "All right, let's finish up," she said. "We want to get to bed early tonight. Tomorrow is a big day."

By the time the next day dawned, more rain had turned the jumper ring into a soupy swamp worse than the day before. Even before the first horse set foot on course, the experts were predicting a day of faults and spills.

The first few competitors didn't prove them wrong. Horses floundered on the shifting footing, bringing down rails, skidding around turns, and sometimes refusing to jump. By the time Snowman was called, there had already been two nasty falls. Nobody had posted a clean round yet, though a horse called Kimberton Vike was in the lead with only two faults.

Harry trotted Snowman through the gate and circled at a slow canter, giving the gelding a chance to find his footing. The big gray shook his head, impatient with the snug hold Harry was keeping on him. As soon as Harry turned him toward the first jump, Snowman was off, splashing through puddles and soaking the unlucky spectators closest to the rail.

His long stride quickened as he closed on the first obstacle, a four-foot-six-inch high gate filled with brush. His ears were pricked as he reached his takeoff spot; his forelegs lifted and tucked, his head and neck stretched forward, and his hind legs pushed him hard and fast off the soggy ground. He leaped over, landing without so much as a skid, and Harry smiled.

On they went, up and over the next jump, and the next. Snowman and Harry made it look as easy in the deep mud as it would have been on dry footing. They sailed over a five-foot gate, a painted wall, a wide brush-and-rail. Aside from one touch that gave him half a fault, Snowman jumped everything flawlessly.

The crowd whooped and applauded as Snowman trotted out splashing up mud with every sure stride. Harry loosened his reins, letting the horse go at his own speed.

"Nice riding, Harry!" someone shouted as they rode past.

Harry tipped his hat at the speaker and then gave Snowman a pat. "Sounds like you've won over the crowd, Teddy Bear," he murmured to the horse.

As Harry had said, Snowman had suddenly become the favorite. Sonoro was already out of the running, and the only one left who could beat the big gray was Oak Ridge's other entry, First Chance. She'd been the favorite coming into the show, and a few people still thought she could take the blue ribbon.

But they were wrong. First Chance turned in a solid performance, but she still ended up three points behind Snowman. Harry rode the big gray back into the muddy ring to accept their ribbon, grinning as if his face might break in two.

The crowd roared with approval as Snowman was announced as the division champion. Snowman lifted his head proudly, gazing out at his fans as if he understood exactly why they were cheering. That only made everyone shout even louder, waving and laughing and talking about the funny-looking gray horse who'd bested the best.

And Harry couldn't have been prouder.

CHAPTER 15

Headlines and Hardships

THAT AFTERNOON, HARRY AND HIS FAMILY PACKED up for the long drive home. They were all in a good mood. Snowman watched them, his head hanging out over his stall door and his eyes sleepy, looking every bit the old plow horse.

All the deLeyers were already thinking ahead past the next few weeks' shows—all the way to Madison Square Garden and the prestigious National Horse Show.

"They'll put a swell blanket on him at the Garden when they bring him out," Chef said dreamily.

Harriet nodded. "He'll get a real trophy, I bet, not just a ribbon."

"Maybe two," Chef declared.

"And a lot of money." Harriet danced over to Snowman's stall and patted the gray's cheek.

Harry had just gone to back the trailer around. He poked his head out of the window, shouting, "Clear the way!"

Harriet and Chef jumped aside. Marty, who had been lying on a hay bale, hopped off. He was eager to be on the way home, especially since Harry had promised to stop for hamburgers along the way.

Chef turned to watch his mother removing the ribbons Snowman and Night Arrest had won, which she'd hung on the wall near their show stalls.

"Before we're through, we'll have enough ribbons to cover that wall," he predicted.

"Two walls." Harriet skipped toward the truck, thinking more now about hamburgers than ribbons.

After the Fairfield show came Lakeville, and after that, Snowman finally began to make headlines. In those days horse showing received regular coverage in the sports pages of all the newspapers—and sometimes on the front pages, as well. Sportswriters debated hotly about the top competitors at the big shows, and fans eagerly followed the standings throughout the season. On July 21, the *New York Times* announced that Harry deLeyer's Snowman, an odd-looking gray gelding, had carried off the open jumper honors at the Lakeville Open Horse Show.

Other papers carried stories about Snowman too. Each sportswriter seemed eager to retell the gray gelding's story, from his humble beginnings to his recent triumphs. They called him "deLeyer's Eighty-Dollar Horse" and "Fugitive from a Cannery" and "the Cinderella Horse." A running argument even developed between Marie Lafrenz of the *New York Herald Tribune* and George Coleman of the *Sun*. Marie was a Snowman fan. She loved the big gray gelding and believed in him. George was willing to admit that Snowman was quite a horse, but he doubted Snowman's ability to come through the grueling circuit with enough left to win at the Garden.

Other writers contented themselves by saying that Harry deLeyer and Snowman kept on winning ribbons that they shouldn't. They said that the former junior Olympic rider and his eighty-dollar horse were not working according to the book.

By the time the deLeyers arrived in Brookville for the next show, everyone seemed to be talking about Snowman. But Harry wasn't feeling as good as he should have been. That was because the sore spot on his tongue was still bothering him—in fact, it was worse than ever. He had trouble eating anything but soup and other soft foods. That took its toll on his body—along with long, tiring days in the saddle—and he grew weak and jumpy.

But there was no time to see a doctor, even if Harry's stubborn pride hadn't stood in the way. Snowman was piling up points week after week, winning championships at shows all over the region. After Brookville came other shows, and at last, Harry felt all his dreams were coming true—all thanks to Snowman.

The week before the Branchville horse show, Harry was hardly able to eat anything at all. His tongue was swollen, and he was in constant pain. He felt weak and shaky as he loaded Snowman onto the trailer, but did his best to hide it from his family. There was no way they could stop now. Not when Snowman was on a winning streak like this one!

A few times Harry thought about asking someone else to ride the big gray, but he always shook the thought from his mind as quickly as it came. Nobody but Harry had ridden Snowman in competition, and over all those shows, the pair had developed a stronger bond than ever. Harry barely had to think about what he wanted on the course before the horse was doing it. Putting anyone else in the saddle—even an accomplished show rider—would throw things off. Harry had seen it happen before. Even the finest jumper might suddenly lose his timing, his feel for height and distance, his ability to adjust his stride to the take-off spot. No, Harry wasn't willing to take that chance.

Branchville was shaping up to be almost as rainy as the Fairfield show had been. On the first day, Harry and

Snowman faced a wet and muddy course, and thick gray clouds threatened more rain soon.

Snowman handled the footing as easily as ever, but the first round still didn't go very well, ending with multiple faults. Harry blamed himself; his timing was off due to pain and weakness, and he wasn't able to give the horse much help on the course. Still, he did his best to ignore the pain as they prepared for the next round later that evening.

Black clouds were already rolling in as the class started. And just as Harry and Snowman rode in through the gate, the sky was torn open by lightning, thunder shook the stands, and sheets of rain came pelting down. Many spectators scurried for shelter, covering their heads with programs. Only a few hardy souls remained to see Snowman jump.

The course was mottled with puddles, and Harry squinted to see through sheets of rain as Snowman picked up a canter. They headed for the first jump, a high brush-and-rail. Snowman soared over and landed with a splash, his big hooves sending dirty water showering up and over himself and his rider. Harry shook his head to clear his vision, giving the big horse his head as he aimed him at the next fence, a tall vertical. He felt weaker than ever and was starting to realize that this round was all up to Snowman. It would be all Harry could do to stay in the saddle and point the horse toward the correct jumps. He did just that, hoping for the best.

And Snowman didn't falter. As they approached the vertical, the big gray galloped on at what seemed to those watching to be a slow pace. That was the way he usually did it, seeming to know that he had the power to make the jump without a furious burst of speed.

But this time he picked up the pace a few strides out, possibly considering the deep puddle right in front of the jump. He found his spot with no input from Harry, tucking his knees as he prepared to push off. . . .

At that moment another ragged bolt of lightning slashed through the rain. Every light in the ring instantly went dark, plunging the course into a thick ocean of blackness.

Harry gasped, leaning forward and preparing himself for a bad spill. But he felt Snowman's hind feet hit the puddle and find the solid ground beneath, hock-deep. Then Snowman pushed off—up, up, up . . .

Later, Harry would say that he was sure the old boy had jumped seven feet over that fence. At the time, all he could do was hang on as they arced through the darkness.

Snowman landed running, plunging ahead into the black rain. A second later a flash of lightning revealed the next jump a few yards ahead. Harry reeled in the reins, trying to slow the big horse, to swing him off course. After all, Snowman didn't have infrared vision, and they were closing in fast on an imposing four-foot-nine-inch tall wall. . . .

Suddenly, the lights blinked back on, and Harry gasped.

But Snowman didn't hesitate, flinging himself over the wall without breaking stride.

A roar went up from the small crowd of soggy spectators. They'd been expecting to see the results of a crash, but instead, they'd seen Snowman jumping as calmly as if it were a bright, dry day! Everyone watching was glad he or she had braved the rain and stayed to see that amazing sight.

Snowman continued on, jumping high and clear over the course, drenching himself and Harry with every stride. He shook the rain from his face, ears pricked forward at each jump. The spectators could tell that the big gray horse was enjoying himself. By the time he finished with a clear round, he was a muddy mess. But his expression was calm and happy as he walked out through the gate.

Harry was just glad to have survived the ride without getting in Snowman's way. But later in the show, things didn't go so well. Harry was so weak that he could hardly climb into the saddle. And during the final round, the big gray knocked down rails and ended with so many faults that he finished out of the ribbons for the first time. Harry blamed himself and knew that if things went on this way, he could ruin Snowman's chance at a national championship. It was a gloomy drive home as he brooded over what to do.

By the time he arrived back at Hollandia, Harry had decided two things: He'd go to the doctor as Johanna had wanted him to do. And he'd ask his friend Dave Kelly to help him find someone to ride Snowman at the show in Smithtown the following weekend.

He called Dave right away, explaining about his health problems in words slurred by his badly swollen tongue. When he finished, there was a moment of silence before Dave finally spoke.

"You can't take that horse out of competition now," he told Harry. "I'll ride him."

Harry was surprised. He'd intended to ask Dave's advice on which local riders he thought could do the best job with the big gray jumper. But he'd never expected Dave to offer to take on the ride himself!

"But you're riding Andante in the jumper stake at Smithtown," he said.

"No reason why I can't ride both." Dave laughed. "If you care to risk it, that is."

Harry smiled. Andante was Dave's pride and joy; he was probably the only rider who could have turned the unpredictable mare into a reliable champion. But Harry had known Dave for years and knew he was an honest competitor.

"It would be no risk," he said. "You've never held a horse back in your life."

"Thanks." Dave sounded pleased. "Then it's settled."

After he hung up, Harry still wasn't sure this new plan

was going to work. But if anyone could get a decent ride out of the big gray, it was Dave Kelly. He was perhaps the best professional rider in this part of the country.

Harry did his best to put it out of his mind for the moment, and went to the doctor. After a brief exam, the doctor led him into his office for a talk.

He made a few notes on his pad and then looked up at Harry. "You have a tumor," he told him. "It will have to come out at once. I'll make arrangements at the hospital. You won't have to stay there, but you'll need to rest for a few days after the procedure."

"A tumor?" Harry stared at the doctor, trying to take in this shocking news. "Then it could be serious?"

"Yes," the doctor admitted. "But let's not borrow trouble. I'll send some of the tissue to the laboratory, and we'll see what they say."

He took a sample of the tumor and sent Harry home to wait for his operation. Not wanting to upset Johanna until he knew more, he told her only that he had to go to the hospital to have the growth on his tongue removed. He said he wanted to get it over with so he could get back to riding Snowman.

The operation happened that Tuesday, and it went quickly and smoothly. When it was over, Harry's mouth was sore, but he felt better with the tumor gone.

After a few hours' rest, his doctor came in to tell him

he could go home. Johanna was there and was relieved to hear it.

"Get this filled," the doctor told Harry, handing him a prescription. "Rest and try to eat as much solid food as you can. I'll be in touch as soon as I receive the laboratory report."

Johanna's eyes widened, and she turned to stare at the doctor. Harry hadn't told her anything about a laboratory report. Did that mean something serious was going on?

Before she could ask, the doctor headed for the door. "And don't ride again until I've checked you over, Harry," he called over his shoulder.

Harry and Johanna didn't have much to say to each other on the way to the drugstore. For one thing, Harry's mouth was bandaged, and it wasn't easy to talk. When they did say a few words, it was mostly about Snowman. Harry was planning to keep a close watch on the gelding's progress with Dave Kelly riding him. He was a little jealous that the other man would get to take Snowman into the ring at the Smithtown show.

He gazed out the car window as they turned in past the gate at Hollandia Farm. "I feel better already," he told his wife. "I'll be riding that big boy by the time of the Stony Brook show."

"And Snowman will be back winning," Johanna said. She reached over to squeeze Harry's arm, hoping that nothing would happen to ruin their glorious summer or Snowman's campaign to the championship.

For the next three days, Harry tried to rest as the doctor had ordered. But it was hard for him to stay away from the horses—especially Snowman. He couldn't stop thinking about the coming show. None of the other horses from Hollandia would be competing at Smithtown, and Harry knew that Dave Kelly would give Snowman the best ride he could. But would it be good enough? Harry couldn't help feeling that nobody else would be able to get as much out of the gray gelding as he could.

On Saturday, Harry and Johanna returned to the doctor's office for his follow-up appointment. After only a few minutes in the waiting room, the nurse ushered them both into the doctor's office. Harry was surprised. He'd been expecting to go to the examination room first.

The doctor was waiting for them behind his desk, a professional smile on his face.

"Good morning, Johanna, Harry." He nodded toward the guest chairs. "Please be seated." As they obeyed, he pulled a sheet of paper toward himself and studied it, a small frown playing around his lips. He took a deep breath and looked up. "Do you have anyone who can take charge of your affairs, Harry?"

Harry was silent for a moment, puzzled. "No," he said. "Why do you ask?"

The doctor glanced down at the paper again. "I received the report on the tissue from your tongue," he said. "It arrived just an hour ago."

"Yes?" Harry said.

The doctor cleared his throat, glancing from Harry to Johanna and back again. "The tumor was malignant."

CHAPTER 16

Terrible News

HARRY AND JOHANNA STARED AT THE DOCTOR FOR several long seconds, unable to process what he'd just said. Finally, Harry blurted out a single word: "Cancer?"

"I'm afraid so." The doctor nodded. "I'll have to operate again—the sooner the better. I'd like to have it done within three days."

"How—how serious is it?" Johanna managed to blurt out at last. The dreaded word "cancer" had shocked her into a state of numbness. But both she and Harry came from strong, hardy Dutch stock, and her courage was already returning.

"I'll have to take more than half the tongue to make sure we remove all the malignant cells," the doctor said.

"What will that mean?" Harry asked.

The doctor regarded him somberly. "You won't be able

to speak normally," he replied. "In time, however, you'll learn to communicate in a limited way. And there will need to be plenty of follow up to make sure we've removed all the malignant cells. You'll be under my close care for quite a while."

"I can't go on with the horse farm, then?" Harry asked.

The doctor shook his head. "I'm afraid not. You won't be up to that kind of work anymore."

Harry climbed slowly to his feet. "All right," he said dully. "I'll report to the hospital in three days."

"Everything will be ready." The doctor stood too, watching Harry with concern. "I'll have a specialist come in to assist, of course."

Harry merely nodded. Then he turned and left the office with Johanna right behind him. She put a hand on his arm as they walked across the parking lot, still trying to take in what had just happened.

As they got into the car, the realization finally struck them both like a massive blow. This was the end of the life Harry deLeyer had always known, the end of Hollandia Farm, the end of his job at the Knox School. And of course, the end of Snowman's quest for glory.

Finally, they started talking, because there were many decisions to make, many things that would have to be done very quickly. They talked about selling the horses. Snowman was, of course, an asset that would bring in quite a nice sum of money—nothing like the amount he would sell for after winning a national championship, but still a large amount.

"I'll call Oak Ridge Stables tomorrow," Harry said. "I'm sure they'd love to own Snowman."

He stared out the window, trying to imagine life without the big, easygoing gray gelding. It was hard—almost harder than all the rest.

"It's too bad Chef isn't older," Johanna said. "Then he could take over."

Harry merely nodded. He'd had the same thought himself. But Chef wouldn't be ready for many years. Neither of them suggested that Johanna be the one to go on with the horse farm, even though she was a fairly experienced horsewoman in her own right. If things didn't go well after the operation, Harry would need her care. Besides, there were four young children to look after.

Harry sighed, turning his mind to what other ways there might be to keep his family going once the farm and his job at the school were gone. But it was hard to make those sorts of plans before the next operation, and so his thoughts crept back to Snowman. They had been so close! So close to fulfilling Harry's lifelong dream. So close to proving that the big gray had what it took to be a national champion.

Now somebody else would get to prove that. Perhaps it was for the best that Snowman would be carrying a different rider at the Smithtown show. It would help get him used to his new life. It was just too bad that Harry wouldn't get to ride him one last time, win one last competition. . . .

Harry continued to stare out the window. They were about halfway home by now.

He turned to Johanna. "Let's go to Smithtown and watch the show," he said.

"I'd like that," Johanna replied. She had a feeling that watching Snowman jump might be just what Harry needed right now to take his mind off the situation. It might be just what she needed too. She wasn't looking forward to breaking the news to the children, especially Chef and Harriet.

As they turned and headed toward Smithtown, their talk returned to selling off the horses. Harry was sure that plenty of people would be interested in Wayward Wind, who had been doing very well at the shows all summer. Another upcoming star was a young horse known as Pedro. He had good bloodlines, but had been a slow developer. Harry had picked him up cheap from his previous owners, who hadn't considered him worth the work of training for a career as a show horse. Johanna had taken to the lanky colt at once, turning him into her own special training project under Harry's watchful eye. Now, Pedro was filled out and coming along nicely, attracting plenty of attention at the shows. He would be an easy sale too.

There was Night Arrest, of course, whose owner would

have to find a new stable and trainer for the spirited mare. And the other boarders would have to be told to find other homes for their horses.

Then there were the riding horses and the ponies, the ones who gave lessons or were rented out for hacks. They might take longer to sell and weren't likely to bring in much money. It was depressing to imagine them all leaving Hollandia, climbing into trailers and trundling away forever.

Amid such thoughts, Harry and Johanna finally reached the showgrounds. They found a place in the bleachers overlooking the main ring, avoiding the few people they knew in the crowd. Harry made no attempt to go down to the warm-up area to see Snowman. His grooms were there, taking good care of the big gray horse. And Harry knew he might as well get used to not seeing Snowman before a competition, to not handling him and talking to him, scratching his neck to make him roll up his lip. . . . There were a hundred small things he'd have to get used to missing. The only thing he might still be able to do was exactly what he was doing now—sitting in the stands among strangers, watching the big gray horse from a distance.

He didn't have much time to brood over that before the open jumper event began. As Harry watched the horses emerge one by one for their rounds, a hard lump formed in his throat. Jumpers had been his life for so long, and soon, that life would be over. He wasn't sure he could bear it. But he seemed to have little choice.

When Andante came out for her turn, he leaned forward to watch. The beautiful mare pranced through the gate as usual, with Dave Kelly handling her expertly. He turned her toward the first jump, and she cleared it gracefully.

"Lovely," Johanna murmured, and Harry nodded.

The rest of Andante's round went well. She finished with only two faults.

"Snowman will have to be at his best to beat her," Harry said.

"Yes," Johanna agreed. They were both thinking the same thing. With Harry in the saddle, the big gray could certainly do it. But would he perform as well for someone else?

When Snowman's turn came, he trotted through the gate in his usual easy manner. Dave Kelly turned him to begin his circle. Despite his firm rein, Snowman twisted his head around to look at the people standing along the ring fence, as he always did. Then the gray gelding turned his eyes upward, gazing into the bleachers, as if searching for a familiar face.

Johanna took a deep breath and clenched her hands in her lap. Harry leaned forward even farther, his eyes on the big gray, resisting the urge to call out Snowman's name.

Finally, Dave got Snowman turned around, and they

headed for the first jump. Harry held his breath. He wanted Snowman to turn in a good round on this, his last time carrying the deLeyer name.

The first fence went well, with Snowman arcing up and over easily, not even coming close to touching a rail. Dave aimed him at the next fence, and Harry could tell that his friend was riding as closely as possible to the way Harry himself always rode the big gelding—giving him a light rein, stretching forward along his muscular neck, letting him take over at each jump.

And it was working! Snowman cleared the coop, the wall, the brush-and-rail, and all the rest. He jumped high and easy and clean, galloping on to a clear victory in the class. When Dave pulled him up at the end, he was grinning, and the crowd cheered wildly.

In the stands, Harry smiled, not bothering to add to the cheers. His palms were damp, and he felt a great emptiness inside him. But he was grateful to Dave Kelly for riding Snowman so well—riding to win, even over his own cherished Andante.

He turned to Johanna. "I guess we can go now," he said.

As they started to rise, the public address system crackled to life. "Attention!" the announcer said. "Mr. Harry deLeyer is wanted at home at once. An emergency at the home of Mr. Harry deLeyer."

CHAPTER 17

More News

AS THEY RUSHED OUT OF THE BLEACHERS TO THEIR car, Harry and Johanna were too anxious to talk. Terrible thoughts ran through their heads. What had happened at home? Was one of the children sick or injured? Had there been a fire? How much more bad luck could strike the family?

In those days there were no cell phones, and they didn't bother to search for a pay phone. It seemed best to rush home as quickly as they could. Soon, they were roaring along the highway in the station wagon, driving as fast as they dared.

When they turned in through the gate at Hollandia Farm, Harry was relieved to see no sign of a fire. In fact, everything in the yard and stable appeared peaceful.

"Where are the children?" Johanna wondered anxiously.

Harry shook his head. None of the children were anywhere in sight.

Johanna jumped out of the car as soon as it stopped, racing for the house. Harry was right behind her. The kitchen door stood open, and they burst inside without slowing.

The neighbor woman was washing dishes at the sink and let out a squawk of surprise. "Oh!" she exclaimed, spinning around to face Harry and Johanna. "You startled me!"

"The children!" Johanna cried. "Where are they?"

"Down in the playroom," the neighbor said calmly. She looked at Harry. "There was a call from your doctor. He said it was urgent and for you to call him as soon as you came in."

"That's wonderful!" Johanna blurted out, relieved that the children were safe.

Realizing what she'd said, she shot her husband an apologetic look. He smiled and nodded, completely understanding what she meant.

"We've had all the bad news that doctor can give us," Harry said. "I wonder what else he's come up with that's such an emergency?"

He walked into the living room and sat down beside the phone. Then he searched his pockets for the card with the doctor's number on it. Now that he knew the children and farm were safe, all the urgency had drained out of him. Still, he supposed he'd better see what the doctor wanted. Perhaps the time of the operation had changed, or there was some other detail that Harry would need to know.

Johanna stood in the doorway. She wanted to go down to the playroom to check on the children, but she also wanted to know why the doctor had called.

Finally, Harry located the number. "This is Harry deLeyer," he said when the receptionist answered. "I understand the doctor wishes to speak to me."

"Mr. deLeyer? Yes!" The receptionist sounded oddly excited. "I'll put the doctor on at once."

Harry frowned and waited, not understanding the receptionist's eager tone. A moment later the doctor came on the line.

"Harry?" The doctor sounded excited too. "Good news!"

"Yes?" Harry said. "What is it?"

"The laboratory made a mistake!" the doctor exclaimed. "They got your tissue analysis mixed up with another report. Your tumor was benign!"

Harry sat staring at the phone. Seeing the blank look on his face, Johanna rushed over to him.

"Did you hear me, Harry?" the doctor said. "You do not have a malignant tumor!"

"I heard you," Harry said at last. "Thanks." He dropped the receiver into place and slowly turned to face Johanna.

"What is it?" Johanna demanded, sick with worry.

She was startled when Harry suddenly started to laugh. Then he stopped and jumped to his feet. "I don't have cancer," he said. "The lab sent my doctor somebody else's tissue report." His smile momentarily faded. "Tough on somebody," he added.

"You don't have cancer?" Johanna echoed.

For a long moment they stood staring at each other. It was hard to believe what had just happened. This was something that could only take place in real life; no storyteller would dare use such a fantastic, nearly unbelievable, plot twist.

"You don't have cancer," Johanna whispered again.

"I don't have a thing wrong with me," Harry said. "I feel wonderful."

They smiled at each other, the numbness that had taken hold within them melting away, replaced by a surge of joy. They collapsed into each other's arms, overwhelmed at the happiness of having their lives—their future—given back to them.

CHAPTER 18
Moving Forward

HARRY'S TONGUE HEALED FAST, AND HE THREW HIM-self back into his work with renewed vigor. It felt good to ride Snowman again, and the big gelding seemed happy to have Harry back in the saddle too. Everyone at Hollandia was looking forward to Snowman's next competition at Stony Brook.

"September fifth," Chef said to Snowman as he brushed the big gray after a ride. "That's when we go."

Harry smiled at his son and the horse. Snowman was jumping better than ever, and Harry was looking forward to getting back in the show ring with him. And since his cancer scare, he'd discovered that others felt the same way. When Dave Kelly had ridden Snowman at Smithtown, word had got around that Harry deLeyer was seriously ill. Afterward, calls had poured in from all over the area, and

Harry and Johanna had explained the situation over and over again. The result was that Harry discovered that he was better known than he'd realized—and well liked, too. He also learned that Snowman had a host of friends who wanted to see him go on and win.

Nearly losing the chance to help him do that had made Harry more determined than ever. Points became almost an obsession; he spent every spare moment figuring out how many Snowman had already earned as well as how many more he needed to qualify for the various year-end prizes. He wanted to enter Madison Square Garden with at least one national honor already in the bag—namely, the Professional Horsemen's Association of America's trophy, known as the PHA.

But that required more showing, and Harry considered himself lucky that Snowman was such a hardy horse, well suited to the rigors of jumping high fences week after week. He also appreciated how little work it took to keep the big gray happy. Nobody ever had to soothe any temperamental outbursts or fits of nervousness. Snowman didn't need hours of work to keep him from getting restless or bored or nasty. All he required was attention from Harry and the children, and the chance to gallop around and kick up his heels once in a while.

Or so Harry thought before Stony Brook, anyway.

• • •

The first day of the Stony Brook show couldn't have gone better for Harry. He began by winning a knock-down-and-out class with Night Arrest against a very strong field. The willful mare was as ornery as ever, and Harry had to ride hard to keep her in check. But she performed spectacularly, and Harry was proud of how far she'd come.

Snowman did well that first day too. When he entered the ring for the open jumper stake, his small ears were pricked, and he tossed his head playfully at the crowd. The responding applause was deafening; by this point, Snowman was definitely the crowd favorite. And he put on a great show for his fans, winning the class easily.

But toward the end of the show, things changed. Harry had entered Snowman in a knock-down-and-out class, and things started off well enough. But when they approached a triple-bar jump partway through the course, Snowman hesitated on his approach. His powerful hind end sprang off the ground as smoothly as ever, but his timing was off, and his hooves crashed into the top rail, sending it flying and eliminating him from the competition.

At first, Harry wasn't too concerned. "That was no good, big fellow," he told Snowman as he rode back to the stabling area. "I think you're getting too used to winning all the time. You can't take any jump for granted—makes you careless."

Snowman's ears swiveled, listening to Harry's voice. But

his steps were heavy and slow. And when Harry unsaddled him by the stalls, he noticed that the big gray horse was sweating much more than he should have been. He placed a hand on Snowman's chest and felt a trembling beneath the skin.

"What happened?" Chef cried breathlessly, skidding into view with his sister at his heels.

"Careless Snowman!" Harriet scolded, shaking a finger in the horse's face.

"No, I think there's something wrong." Harry waved at Chef. "Fetch me the thermometer from the first-aid kit at once."

Both children went silent and solemn. Chef rushed off, returning shortly with the thermometer. Nobody said a word as Harry took the horse's temperature.

"Normal," Harry said with relief as he read the results.

He tossed a cooler over the horse's back and walked him until he stopped sweating and trembling. After that, Snowman appeared to return to normal. But Harry remained worried. Had the frenzied pace of that summer's show schedule finally caught up to Snowman? Had the big gray's placid and willing temperament hidden it until it was too late? Harry hoped not; this was a critical period of time if he wanted to stay in the hunt for the year-end honors. Harry hated the thought of backing off now. But he had to do what was right for Snowman.

When they arrived back at Hollandia Farm, Harry left

the other horses to the grooms and focused on Snowman. He'd been thinking about what to do and had decided against calling the vet. He knew the big gray horse like the back of his hand, and Harry was pretty sure that it wasn't medicine that Snowman needed. Just rest. As much as it took, no matter the consequences.

Trying not to think about what that might mean, Harry carefully wrapped Snowman's legs and then put him in his stall with plenty of hay and bedding.

"Good night, you big teddy bear," he said, scratching the horse's neck until Snowman's lip jutted out. "Rest up. You've earned it."

Harry tossed and turned for a long time that night before falling asleep. He hated the thought of giving up on his dream of winning a national championship with Snowman. But if Snowman was too tired to go on, Harry wouldn't push him. That wouldn't be fair. Still, it would be hard to give up that dream. . . .

Finally, he fell asleep. He woke up feeling groggy, and looked out the window. It was bright daylight— Harry had overslept. He got up and dressed quickly, wanting to check on Snowman right away.

He was headed for the back door when there was a knock. One of the grooms was outside, looking excited.

"Snowman!" the young man exclaimed.

Harry was still feeling groggy and unsettled. "Is he down?" he asked tersely, fearing the worst.

"Down?" The groom laughed. "No, I just saw him out in the paddock taking a jump! He sure looked funny doing it in his stable bandages and sheet."

Harry blinked at him, not understanding for a moment. Then his face relaxed into a grin. Apparently, Snowman had just had a bad day yesterday. And now the big gray horse had decided his rest—short as it had been—was over.

CHAPTER 19

Piping Rock

PIPING ROCK STARTED ON SEPTEMBER 12 THAT YEAR.
The big prestigious show would be the toughest test yet for
Snowman. It would also be the last show of the summer
before Chef and Harriet went back to school. That made it
feel extra special, even though attending shows was old hat
by then for the deLeyer clan.

There was plenty to do to get settled in. During that
same time, the family discussed Snowman's competition.
The field for the open jumper division included not only
his old rival, Andante, but other big names from all across
the country. There were the experienced jumpers Diamant
and Ksar d'Esprit, who had both been named to the United
States Equestrian Team that spring and competed all over
Europe that summer. There was a well-known champion
from Virginia called Smithereens, at least one successful

jumper that had shipped in all the way from California, and others.

Most of the local sportswriters favored Diamant to win. He had the most experience and was in top form after his successful campaign that summer. But Harry and his family held a different opinion, and so did many of Snowman's fans!

"There we are," Johanna said as she tacked the last of Snowman's many ribbons onto the wall by his stall. "Now he looks like a proper champion."

Chef rushed over to look. "I hope you left space for the one he's going to win here," he said.

His mother smiled. "Don't worry. I'll make room."

Harry hurried in, straightening his show jacket, which he'd just put on. His boots were shined, and he looked calm and ready to go.

"Is all the hay stacked?" he asked the children.

Chef nodded. "It's done. And the grain sack is tied shut so nothing can get into it."

"Yes, everything is done." Harriet sounded a bit impatient. "But shouldn't we get Snowman tacked up? It's almost time!"

Harry chuckled and tousled his daughter's blonde hair. "I'll take care of that," he said. "You'd better go out and find a good place on the fence to watch. I imagine it's getting crowded out there."

In the first open jumper round of the day, only two horses ended up going clear over the tough Olympic level course: Diamant and Snowman. The two of them moved on to the second round.

When Snowman entered for his turn, he pricked his ears toward the jumps, clearly noticing that they had been raised. Harry smiled, feeling the big gray's eagerness. He'd always liked the higher jumps better!

Snowman went clear again, to the delight of the crowd. When it was Diamant's turn, the keen bay turned in a good performance—but ended with one fault.

That meant Snowman was in the lead for the championship and the Blitz Gold Cup, which was awarded based on the total points earned in all of the open jumper classes at the show.

The second round of open jumpers featured an even tougher course. Nobody expected any horse in the field to go clean, but two of them did. This time, Snowman's only competition in the second round was Oak Ridge's champion, Sonoro. Sonoro hadn't competed on the previous day and was much fresher than Snowman. That worried Harry, but he trusted the big gray to let him know if he couldn't handle it.

Snowman was the first to tackle the higher jump-off course. Harry rode carefully, guiding his mount around and helping him in any way he could. Snowman felt good—but on the very last jump, Snowman misjudged his distance and knocked down a rail for four faults. Harry's heart sank, but he rubbed Snowman's neck.

"Good job, Snowman," he said.

Sonoro was being piloted by Oak Ridge's talented rider Adolph Mogavero. Adolph looked confident as he rode in and got started. Sonoro took the jumps eagerly, with the swift grace he was known for. But he too collected four faults over the final obstacle. Sonoro and Snowman were still tied.

That meant the rails would go up again for another jump-off. But this would be the final round, which meant time would count. If the horses ended up equal in faults again, the fastest round would win.

That settled the issue for many of those watching. Against the fleet Sonoro, Harry's big gray farm horse, who never seemed to exert himself, wouldn't stand a chance. It was the same situation Harry and Snowman had faced at the Fairfield show, when Harry had bowed out to save the horse's energy.

But Harry wasn't giving up this time. They needed to win this class to stay in the lead for the Blitz Gold Cup. As he rode into the ring and looked over the course, Harry understood that he'd have to use every riding trick he knew to save time. He and Snowman would need to make up for their lack of speed by cutting corners; there could be no wide sweeping turns and long approaches to set up for each jump.

Harry put his plan into action beginning at the first jump. As Snowman landed on the far side, he firmly pulled Snowman's head around in the direction of the second jump. As they veered over and closed on it, he leaned forward along the sturdy gray neck and spoke to Snowman: "High, boy, high!"

Snowman cleared the fence and pounded on, zigzagging his way around the course at Harry's direction. At the brush-and-rail, which loomed extra high and wide, Harry spoke to the horse again: "Up, Teddy Bear, up!"

Snowman put his heart into the jump, but one foot struck the fence, giving him a fault. Harry knew what that meant—if Sonoro went clear, he would be the winner.

But he might not go clear, and so, Harry pushed Snowman forward still faster, careening around the next turn to the final line of jumps. Snowman lumbered into high gear, like a farm horse headed to the barn after a long day's work in the fields. But the speed cost him—by the time he leaped over the final jump, he had collected a total of four faults on the course. Harry slumped in the saddle and gave the horse a pat, knowing they'd done their best.

Adolph Mogavero guided Sonoro through the gate and swung toward the first fence. Watching from outside the ring, Harry could almost read the calculation in the other rider's eye. Should he keep Sonoro at an easy pace, which would give him a better chance at ending with fewer faults than Snowman? Or let him out to his full speed, which could cost a fault or two but would surely beat the bigger, heavier horse?

As soon as he started, Harry could tell that Adolph had chosen to play it safe. He kept Sonoro at an even pace, though even that appeared faster than Snowman's thundering stride.

Harry watched, sure that he and Snowman would have to settle for second place this time. But to his amazement, even the sedate pace didn't save Sonoro's round—a couple of small mistakes meant a final score of four faults—just like Snowman!

Everyone watching seemed to hold their breaths as the judges checked the time sheets. Harry sat stock-still, waiting.

The public address system clicked on. "Harry deLeyer's Snowman: four faults. Time: fifty-four seconds," the announcer said. "Mrs. James Nessler's Sonoro: four faults. Time: fifty-nine seconds."

The crowd went wild, letting out a great roar that went on and on. Harry smiled, relieved that his plan had worked. Snowman had done his part in jumping the challenging course. But it was Harry's skillful riding that had furnished those all-important five seconds!

Now Snowman had an eight-point lead over Diamant heading into the final round of open jumpers. That was a comfortable margin, but not an insurmountable one. Harry knew that the big gray would have to stay sharp if they wanted to win the Blitz Gold Cup.

And the strain of the tough competition was beginning to show in all the horses—and the riders too. It was times like these when horsemen liked to say that breeding and heart would tell. Snowman had no special breeding behind him that anyone knew about, but he had plenty of heart. He managed to rack up points through the first few rounds of the final division, but by the time of the all-important final round, Diamant had taken the lead by five points.

The final course was another challenging one. None of the horses went clean until Snowman walked in—and walked out after posting a perfect round.

But Diamant had yet to compete. He had power equal to Snowman's and a great deal more experience. Did he have equal heart?

He started the course well, jumping with class and finesse. But halfway through, a small mistake led to a rail coming down. And just like that, Snowman had won the championship and the Blitz Gold Cup!

CHAPTER 20

On to the Garden

AFTER PIPING ROCK, LIFE GREW EVEN MORE HECTIC for the deLeyers. The children were back at school, able to attend shows only on weekends—though Harry and Johanna had promised to let them skip school if Snowman reached Madison Square Garden. The press was taking an even greater interest in Snowman, now that the big fall shows were coming. Many of the writers were calling Harry "the Flying Dutchman" and clamoring to interview him. Harry was willing to talk to them, but only so long as it didn't interfere with his work.

And there was plenty to do, as Snowman continued to compete at even farther-flung shows—in Paramus, New Jersey; Harrisburg, Pennsylvania; and Washington, DC. The big gray met and mastered every course. He even won a six-bar jumper class, one of the toughest tests a show jumper could face. The course consisted of six obstacles set in a straight line, with the first jump set at three feet eight inches and the height gradually increasing to five feet. Snowman seemed to enjoy that challenge, thrilling the spectators with his victory.

In fact, Snowman was thrilling crowds wherever he went now. Whenever he trotted into a ring, he received an ovation like no other jumper had known. He even became a bit of a show-off, demonstrating the sense of humor he was famous for by shaking his head at the crowd.

But on course, he was all business. At the very first Washington International Horse Show, held in the nation's capital and with President and Mrs. Eisenhower in attendance, he racked up point after point. His last course of the show was another six-bar class. Only a few horses had entered, since many jumpers couldn't handle that type of tricky, intense course—especially in the muddy conditions that day. But Snowman had proved himself a capable mudder, and Harry wasn't particularly worried about the footing.

The first three horses to go collected faults. Snowman came out fourth, jumping the first few fences easily.

But at the five-foot jump, his hoof hit an especially slick spot and he skidded forward—crashing right through the jump! He struggled to stay on his feet but failed, rolling over in the mud. Harry was thrown clear, though he ended up sore and covered in mud from head to foot.

It was the first time Snowman had ever fallen on course. Harry leaped to his feet, anxious to check on the big gray. By the time he got there, Snowman was already back on his feet. The horse was staring at the wrecked jump, an astonished expression on his face. Then, with a snort, he turned his back on the mess of poles.

Harry grabbed the dangling reins and led him out of the ring, keeping a close eye on Snowman for signs of injury or lameness. But he couldn't see even the slightest limp or hesitation in the horse's steady walk. There was no sign that the fall had shaken him up, either. Snowman seemed just as calm and self-possessed as ever—just muddier!

The seventy-fifth annual National Horse Show was to take place at Madison Square Garden from November 4 to November 11 that year. It would be a grueling eight days of competition, with up to five hundred horses entered in every class. But the deLeyer clan had boundless faith in their eighty-dollar horse.

And so they packed up and set off for New York City. They made their way through the cavernous canyons of the great metropolis, where the bustle and clang of traffic replaced the soft voice of the wind in the tall trees, and the night chorus of pond and stream. Here, instead of croaking frogs and chirping birds, there were only the angry shrill of automobile horns, and the roar and rattle of cars and trains.

Here, there were no bridle paths, just the hard pavement being pounded day and night by rubber tires, for by those days, the streets had long since forgotten the impact of a shod hoof. The quarters where the horses stayed for the show were stuffy and crowded, with none of the fresh country air they'd known all summer and fall.

Still, the deLeyers were happy, excited, and eager to get on with the show. Johanna and Harriet quickly got to work brightening the stall area with the colorful ribbons Snowman had won all season. After tacking them up, they set out stools and the picnic lunch they'd brought. Meanwhile, Chef and Marty tacked up a hand-lettered sign reading SNOWMAN on his stall door.

Harry and the grooms were busy settling the horses in. They scattered the stall floors with deep beds of straw, broke open bales of hay, measured out grain. Nobody found it strange that Harry worked just as hard as the hired grooms. While stables like Oak Ridge, with its twenty-nine grooms, didn't expect trainers or riders to do barn work, the deLeyer operation was a dirty-hands job—everybody pitched in and did what needed to be done.

In addition to Snowman, Harry had brought Night Arrest and also a horse named Belle Amie, who had been coming along strong during the latter part of the season. While Belle Amie and Snowman settled in quickly, Night Arrest was jumpy from the start. The wild little mare didn't like New York City's sounds and smells. Harry watched her pace her stall, rolling her eyes with irritation, and wondered how she'd react to the lights and confinement of the Garden's indoor arena. But he was sure he'd manage to get her around her courses, just as he'd done all along.

Grooms, handlers, and spectators stopped by the stalls regularly to see Snowman, who had become such a sensation during that summer and fall's campaign. Some were curious and just wanted a closer look at the fabulous eighty-dollar horse who'd galloped in from the farm fields to challenge the country's best blue-blooded show horses. But those who knew anything about horses had only to take in Snowman's fine head, with his Arabian ears and intelligent eyes, to recognize that he was a horse to be reckoned with.

Of course, that fact was already well-known to those who had competed against him at previous shows. Many of these riders and trainers stopped by just to offer Harry and Johanna luck and give Snowman himself a friendly pat. He was that kind of horse.

CHAPTER 21

The Big One

THE OPEN JUMPERS WERE SCHEDULED TO START AT eleven a.m. Harry had already taken Snowman to the training ring across the street from the stables to stretch his legs and warm up for the class. The grooms were dealing with the other two horses. Harry was focused on his big gray star. This was the show they'd been working toward all summer and fall, the one that would cement Snowman's place among the greatest champions of the sport. All they had to do was win.

Harry had all the confidence in the world in his horse, but even he knew that winning would be a challenge at this show more than any other. Snowman would face many horses he'd jumped against before, but also many new ones. Oak Ridge Stables's First Chance and Sonoro were both competing, along with Andante. So were Diamant and Ksar d'Esprit. Then there was Saxon Wood, who had won reserve champion at the Garden the year before, and Little David, a small but fiery jumper who had been known to stage a number of upsets. Two of the nation's best-known female riders were out to take the prize away from the men—Betty Bosley on the Clown, and Shirley Weinstein riding Bellaire, a horse who had been a member of the Canadian Equestrian Team. And countless more.

But the list would be winnowed quickly to the top fifteen competitors. And Harry planned to make sure Snowman was among that elite group.

Chef, Harriet, and Marty were hopping with excitement by the time the army band started playing to officially open the day's events. Then the Royal Canadian Mounted Police marched in on their black horses, their scarlet uniforms gleaming under the lights. The children whooped with approval as the Mounties performed an intricate drill and then galloped out.

Finally, though, it was time for the main event. The open jumpers were about to begin.

Horses came into the ring one by one to take the first course. Some of them reacted poorly to the noisy crowd and the indoor ring, with its odd shadows and echoes. Many danced in place or spooked as their riders maneuvered them into position to begin.

But when Snowman's turn came, he trotted in as

placidly as ever. He paused to look around, as he always did, and Harry smiled as he wondered if the big gray was disappointed not to see a line of eager children perched around the edges of the ring.

Plenty of people in the crowd recognized Snowman and Harry. They'd read about the Flying Dutchman and his Cinderella horse in the papers. They roared their approval, and Snowman shook his head playfully at them before getting down to business.

The course was compact with many tight turns. The ring at the Garden was relatively small, so the course designer had laid things out as best he could, asking the horses to crisscross back and forth frequently.

But the tight course gave Snowman little trouble. He cleared all the jumps—verticals, bank, split rails, stone wall—neatly and easily, finishing with only two faults. But Diamant was even better, forcing Snowman to settle for second place in the round.

Harry was disappointed but not dismayed. There were plenty of rounds left to make up those points. He took Snowman back to the stalls and settled him in, giving him a pat for a job well done. Harry and the horses would have a break that afternoon while the international team event took place. His family went to watch the competition, cheering for their favorites. But Marty didn't get really excited until the Budweiser Clydesdales clopped in, pulling a gaily colored beer wagon. Chef and Harriet loved the huge draft horses too, and Johanna smiled, thinking back to the big drafts she'd known years earlier in Holland.

The knock-down-and-out class took place that night at ten p.m. Harry had entered both Snowman and Night Arrest. The little mare was the first of the two to go, and Harry knew from the moment she stepped foot in the ring that he wasn't going to have an easy time with the excitable mare. She hated the lights and the noisy crowd, and the towering stands rising in all directions seemed to terrify her.

Still, Harry managed to wrestle her into some semblance of a canter and aim her at the first fence, a four-foot high brush-and-rail. She skittered forward wildly, all but out of control, but somehow Harry managed to check her at the right moment, and she cleared the jump.

A wave of applause rolled out from the crowd. Night Arrest was an eye-catching horse with obvious class, and besides that, everyone could see that she was giving Harry trouble. Everyone wanted to see what would happen next.

Harry wasn't paying attention to the applause or to anything else except the horse and the next jump. Night Arrest wasn't settling at all; if anything, she was getting worse, fighting the bit and trying to speed up.

Doing his best to stay calm, Harry checked her again. But this time she ignored him, lunging forward right past her take-off spot. In that split second Harry knew the course was over.

Night Arrest crashed into the obstacle. Her head went down, her rump and heels up. She staggered, barely managing to stay on her feet.

Harry fought to keep his seat, but it was no use. He was flung from the saddle, but one foot got stuck in the stirrup. The crowd gasped with horror as the horse took off, dragging Harry like a rag doll.

But Harry gave a yank, freeing his leg and rolling clear. Night Arrest galloped away, head high and eyes rolling with terror.

Harry climbed to his feet and dusted himself off. All his limbs still seemed to be working, so he hurried off after the running mare. With the help of several other people, he finally managed to catch her. The crowd gave him a big hand as he led Night Arrest out of the ring. As far as many of the spectators were concerned, thrills and spills were just part of the show. And at least this time nobody had been hurt.

Minutes later, Harry rode back into the ring, this time aboard Snowman. He was shaken but still confident. Snowman wasn't Night Arrest—the big gray had already been in the claustrophobic indoor ring and handled it just fine. Harry just needed to focus on what they had to do.

Snowman trotted in and shook his head at the crowd.

Then Harry turned him around, and Snowman galloped calmly toward the first jump, clearing it with little fuss. The next few jumps went just as well, but when he reached the triple bars, he came in at a slight angle. One big hind foot touched a rail, which clanked to the ground with a groan from the crowd. That one careless hoof meant their favorite was out of the class.

Harry felt like groaning too. It was the same old story—the triple bars were only four feet six inches. Too easy a jump for Snowman to bother exerting himself.

Back at the stalls, the whole family was gloomy and grim except for Marty, who patted and praised Snowman as if he'd won. Chef frowned at no one in particular.

"We'll show 'em tomorrow," he muttered.

"We have to," Harriet added with a sigh.

Harry said nothing. He knew that one bad day didn't mean a lost cause. They would just have to do better tomorrow.

The next day Snowman took part in another knock-down-and-out class. This time he seemed to want to make up for his bad showing from the night before. He went clean in the first round, along with seven others. Once the rails were raised for a jump-off, only two horses went clean—Snowman and First Chance, one of the stars of Oak Ridge Stables. Adolph Mogavero was riding First

Chance, and Harry knew that Adolph was probably out to even the score after losing to Snowman earlier in the season.

First Chance went clean over the higher course. So did Snowman. That meant another jump-off.

The rails were raised again. In the third round, First Chance started well, but the effort of clearing the enormous jumps began to take its toll. When she reached the fourth jump, she came in short and knocked a rail.

Now all Snowman had to do was go clean, and the class was his. He came back into the ring as calmly as ever. But Harry could sense a subtle change in the horse as he swung into a canter. Snowman felt determined and focused as he picked up speed, hurling himself over one jump after another. By the end the crowd was on its feet. Snowman was back in business—the winner again!

After that second knock-down-and-out class, Snowman was tied with First Chance for the overall championship. But as the show went on, with both horses jumping course after course, First Chance began to pull ahead. On the fifth day, however, Snowman won a tough jump-off to pull within a point of First Chance. Combined with the points Snowman had earned all season, that was enough to win him the US Challenge Trophy as well as the Professional Horsemen's Association trophy. Those were amazing honors, and Harry and his family danced around the stall area gleefully when the announcement was made. But there was one award left, the one Harry had had in his sights all season, the one he really wanted—the US Open Jumper Championship.

CHAPTER 22
End of the Road

GOING INTO THE FINAL EVENT OF THE BIG SHOW, Snowman could boast of two first-place finishes, two seconds, and two thirds. He was still trailing First Chance by a point, but his popularity hadn't waned a bit. The crowd went wild every time he set a hoof inside the arena. Outside of the Garden he was discussed by taxi drivers, waitresses, businessmen, and just about everyone else in the city.

A television producer even called, asking if Snowman would come to his studio on Fifty-Eighth Street. The show would give millions of people a chance to see the farm horse who'd become a jumping star.

In those days, Madison Square Garden was located on Eighth Avenue between Forty-Ninth and Fiftieth Streets, making it a short walk to the TV studio. Harry clipped a lead rope to the gelding's halter, and off they went.

Snowman ambled along Eighth Avenue, attracting plenty of attention. Truck drivers leaned out of their cabs to ask questions or give advice. Taxi drivers slowed down and craned their necks. Pedestrians halted in amazement at the sight of a horse moving along with the flow of traffic. Harry smiled and waved, and Snowman pricked his small ears at people as they passed. They arrived at the studio right on time.

Snowman took the live TV taping in stride. He seemed very interested in the big cameras, the grips, and the boom operators, but he never so much as glanced at his own image on the monitors set up around the studios. As soon as the interview was over, Snowman walked back up Eighth Avenue as sedately as he'd come.

Later, Harry and his family gathered at the gelding's stall to get ready for the final class—the one that would determine the winner of the US Open Jumper Championship. They were tired but happy.

Harry gave Snowman a pat. "When he wins tonight, we'll all go out and accept the award," he told the others with a broad smile.

Chef and Harriet beamed and nodded. Johanna laughed. Marty was more interested in playing with a stick in the dirt.

"It will be quite a procession," Johanna commented.

"Yes." Harry glanced at the children. "And I'll expect you to look your best. Be sure to stay all slicked-up, all right? No messy clothes."

A short while later, Harry and Snowman were warmed up and ready to go. Harry sat on the big horse outside the gate, waiting for Snowman's call. He reached down to scratch the horse's neck. Snowman curled his lip, as always.

"You're going to win, old teddy bear," Harry murmured.

When the call came, the big gray ambled through the gate, then picked up his usual easy trot. Harry waited for the horse to turn and look at the crowd as he always did before asking him to canter. Snowman responded promptly, and they headed toward the first jump.

There had been so many moments like this one; so many eager beginnings to tough courses. And they had all led up to this one. Were they ready?

Snowman pricked his ears toward the brush jump in front of him, his powerful legs swinging him along at a pace that appeared almost lazy to onlookers. Harry leaned forward along the horse's gray neck as Snowman rose and soared over the jump.

"Go, boy, go," he said as they landed, just loudly enough for his voice to reach the horse's small, pricked ears.

And Snowman went. Did he understand that he was galloping for glory, jumping for his spot in history? Probably not, although he was so tuned in to Harry that he may have felt how keyed up he was and sensed that this course was something special.

Up and over—the poles, the coop, the gate, the wall,

the Liverpool, the ditch. All flashed by, well beneath Snowman's big hooves. The crowd started off cheering him on, but as the end of the course neared they fell nearly silent. It was as if everyone in Madison Square Garden was holding their breath, watching the magnificent old plow horse—the magnificent jumper, Snowman—try to win that championship.

Snowman cleared more poles and another wall. Finally, he turned to head for the final jump, five poles over a coop. Bursting with energy and life, he closed in on the obstacle—and cleared it by a foot.

For a long moment the stands remained silent. Then the crowd went wild. The competition wasn't over, but every person watching knew that here was the champion.

And they were right. No other horse came close to matching Snowman's brilliant round. Harry deLeyer's heart was full to bursting as he rode his horse out of the ring and down into the tunnel leading to the stabling area. Once he got there, he leaned forward and patted the solid gray neck and shoulder. He was too overwhelmed to speak, but it didn't matter. No words were necessary between him and Snowman.

Later, the crowd waited impatiently for Harry and Snowman to appear for the trophy presentation. The red carpet was spread, and the officials stood in a line, ready to begin the ceremony.

Snowman appeared in the opening to the tunnel. He was draped in a white blanket, with Harry at his head. Fanned out behind the horse were Marty, Harriet, Chef, and Johanna. The whole group moved sedately toward the waiting officials. The boys wore identical blue jackets, dark pants, and bow ties. Harriet was in a belted dress with a flared skirt and buttons down the front.

The crowd went crazy when they saw them. Harry had to stop Snowman short of the officials until the ovation ended. Snowman pricked his ears, seeming to enjoy the applause.

Then a woman handed Harry the US Championship trophy. The band struck up a lively song and the sudden burst of music seemed to startle Snowman for once in his life. He jerked his head, almost sending the trophy flying, then took several rapid steps back. Harry had his hands full trying to settle him. It was the first time the big gray horse had ever shown any temperament, and the spectators loved it. A roar of laughter went up in the stands, and Harry thought wryly that he'd have to be sure that Snowman would never hear that particular song again.

Snowman had won American Horse Show Association "Horse of the Year," the Professional Horseman's Association Championship, and he was the Champion of Madison Square Garden's Diamond Jubilee. It was the Triple Crown of show jumping. So if Snowman didn't want to hear a particular song, it was the least Harry could do for him.

CHAPTER 23

What Happened After That?

AFTER HIS TRIUMPH AT MADISON SQUARE GARDEN,
Snowman became more of a celebrity than ever. He and
Harry returned to the show ring the following season and
won many more ribbons and accolades. Once again, they
qualified for Madison Square Garden—and once again
came away with both the AHSA and PHA trophies, the first
time a single horse had ever won those championships two
years in a row. Harry and Snowman continued to compete
and win for several more years after that, and Snowman
was later inducted into the Show Jumping Hall of Fame.

But the big gray horse's fame had spread far beyond
the show ring. Fan clubs were formed in his honor, and
everybody knew his name. He was featured in *Life* maga-
zine and *Reader's Digest*, and two books were published
about him in the years after his wins at the Garden,

including the one on which this book is based: *Snowman* by Rutherford Montgomery. Schoolchildren all over the country read Montgomery's book and clamored to meet Snowman. The world-famous horse appeared on several TV shows—Johnny Carson even sat on his back during Snowman's appearance on his popular talk show.

Meanwhile, Harry's success continued. He and Johanna were able to buy a larger property and expand Hollandia Farm, where they trained many horses and Harry taught countless students.

Eventually Snowman retired to this new, larger Hollandia Farm, where he was given his own paddock near the entrance. The enterprising DeLeyer kids took advantage of Snowman's popularity, charging people a small fee to give the big gray horse a pat—at least until Harry found out and put a stop to it!

But mostly, Snowman resumed his status as a family pet and lesson horse. Several more DeLeyer kids learned to ride on him—the family eventually included eight children— and he still taught an occasional lesson to other riders as well. But mostly Snowman lived a life of leisure, relaxing in his paddock and greeting fans who stopped by to visit. In the winter he pulled a sleigh for the deLeyer kids, and in the summer his favorite activity was swimming in the nearby Long Island Sound with them aboard his back. He remained as quiet and good-natured as always, willingly pulling a sled full of giggling kids through the snow or posing for photos with his Arabian ears pricked forward.

Snowman was more than a horse to Harry, Johanna, and the children. He was a true part of the family—from that first snowy afternoon in 1956 until the day he died at the age of twenty-six and was buried on Harry's farm. To this day, Harry DeLeyer knows he was lucky to have Snowman in his life. And that sometimes, eighty dollars can buy you something priceless.

ACKNOWLEDGMENTS

I had the great honor of spending three years with Mr. Harry deLeyer while we were shooting the documentary *Harry & Snowman*, and hearing the amazing story of Snowman first-hand from eighty-five-year-old Harry.

Snowman is as close to his heart today as he was more than forty years ago. Harry's farmhouse in Virginia is a shrine to his old friend, and Harry proudly displays Snowman's original bridle, saddle, championship trophies, and his retirement cooler from Madison Square Garden.

I am grateful to Catherine Hapka for artfully adapting the original 1962 *Snowman*, by Rutherford Montgomery, so that the amazing story of Snowman can live on for generations of young fans.

Ron Davis
Director/Producer, *Harry & Snowman*
www.harryandsnowman.com